Elgar

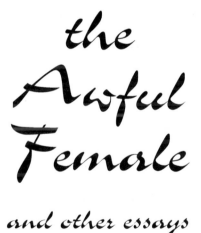

&

the
Awful
Female

and other essays

David B

Elgar Edi

Published in Great Britain by
Elgar Editions

the publishing imprint of

Elgar Enterprises
20 High Street, Rickmansworth, Herts WD3 1ER
(e-mail : editions@elgar.org)

© David Bury, 2003

First Published : April 2003

British Library Cataloguing in Publication Data
A Catalogue record for this book
is available from the British Library

ISBN 0 9537082 6 8 (Elgar Editions)

Printed and bound in Great Britain by
Hobbs the Printers Limited,
Brunel Road, Totton, Hampshire

*Previous page: Elisabeth Scott (below left), architect of the new (1932) Shakespear
Memorial Theatre, with (above right) a contemporary portrait of Sir Edward Elga*

Front cover: The 1932 Shakespeare Memorial Theatre at Stratford;

*Back cover: The original (1879) Shakespeare Memorial Theatre at Stratford, destroye
in a fire in 1926.*

CONTENTS

LIST OF ILLUSTRATIONS

FOREWORD

It is some 25 years since, belatedly, I "discovered" Elgar. I have been trying to catch up ever since. The essays now published comprise six small pieces which resulted from involvement with Elgar in these years. Three were previously published in the *Elgar Society Journal* ('The Potteries Choirmaster' - September 1981; 'The Canadian Carillon' - May 1984; 'Queen Mary's Dolls' House' - July 1999), while 'The Two Mezzos' was given as a presentation to the Society's London Branch and published separately in 1984 by Thames Publishing. Some slight amendment has now been made to these items - for the better, one hopes. The other two essays are published here for the first time.

My gratitude to so many individuals and institutions will be clear from the bibliographies. I am conscious too of how much I owe to so many friends within the Elgar Society with whom I have conversed incessantly about Edward for all these years. However, I am especially indebted to the three Chairmen of the Society's London Branch during my time on the Committee - Diana McVeagh, Maxwell Hutchinson, Martin Passande - and to my predecessor and successor as Branch Secretary - Garry Humphries and D Relf Clark - for all the encouragement and opportunity afforded me. Similarly my debt to Ronald Taylor and Geoffrey Hodgkins who in turn edited the "Journal" in these years is great.

I am grateful, too, to the late Jack McKenzie, Jim Bennett and Chris Bennett of the Elgar Birthplace, and to the Elgar Birthplace Trust for permission to quote the letters of Edward Elgar. Similarly I am indebted to Hersey, Lady Flower, for permission to consult and use the material from the Flower Papers. While every attempt has been made to identify, contact and acknowledge copyright holders, this has not always been possible. The author apologises to any who feel their interests have not been recorded; if they wish to contact him, he will ensure that this omission is rectified in any future reprint.

So far as the business of collating these disparate pieces goes, I owe everything to my fellow Elgarians John Norris and Ann Vernau of Elgar Editions, and to my non-Elgarian colleague Peter O'Brien who insisted that I do something along these lines and then spent hours rendering my ill-typed efforts acceptable. For sure he qualifies for half the famous Hans Richter dedication (1st Symphony) - 'true friend'.

Finally, I am not a musicologist. These essays are for the most part about people and events in Elgar's life. However, few composers put more of 'themselves' into their music, and it seems to me we are unlikely to understand the music unless some attempt is made to know the man. Several of the essays, perhaps, might be thought to show Elgar in a somewhat 'bad light'! Well - though there is no time for a detailed discussion here - he was a very human person, not always easy with himself or others and certainly not consistent in mood. There have been plenty of uncritical memoirs of Elgar and we have long since passed the time when we could be franker. In any case, as Michael Kennedy has pointed out in *Portrait of Elgar:-*

> anybody who spends time among the great collection of letters to Elgar preserved at Worcester will come away with an overwhelming impression of the respect and affection with which he was surrounded.

Quite so! Edward Elgar was not only a genius but also, despite (or perhaps because of) his foibles, a fine man. It has been wonderful to get to know him.

David Bury
March 2003

THE AUTHOR

David Bury was educated at The King's School, Macclesfield and at Leeds and London Universities. He taught History at Grammar Schools in Leeds and Surrey. A member of the Elgar Society since 1979, he was London Branch Secretary from 1984-1995 and has served on the Council of the Elgar Society. He contributed the essay 'Ludwig Wüllner and the Westminster Gerontius' to Elgar Editions' anthology *The Best of Me - A Gerontius Centenary Companion* (Rickmansworth 1999). He has recently completed a study of 'Elgar, A.C.Benson and the Coronation Ode' which, will appear in a planned anthology of London Branch presentations, also to be published by Elgar Editions.

Like mother, like daughter: Once-popular postcard photographs of (above) Marie Brema with (right) her daughter Tita Brand (see pages 12-13), presumably taken at the same photographic session.

ELGAR AND THE TWO MEZZOS

Let me give away the secret straight away. The two mezzos about whom I shall be writing are Marie Brema, immortalised as the original Angel in the ill-fated Birmingham première of *Gerontius* on 3 October 1900, and Muriel Foster, who was undoubtedly to become Elgar's favourite. *Gerontius* provides something of a focus for what I have to say about our two mezzos which, perhaps, comes to a point with the first London performance of 6 June 1903. Of course, short of joining the Chorus, only one of them could sing in the work at a given time, and needless to say there were times, and especially in June 1903, when both wanted so to do. Brema and Foster were not unseemly in their rivalry, but it was none the less real and you may feel there was a clear winner.

Marie Brema was born Minny Feldman in Liverpool of German/American parentage on 28 February 1856. Her stage name of 'Brema' was taken from her father's native city of Bremen in which place, according to Willie Reed, she made her somewhat belated first appearance in 1891. Certainly her English debut took place in February of that year in Schubert's *Ganymede* at a London Popular Concert. In the same year she appeared in Scribe's play *Adrienne Lecouvreur* at Oxford and Harold Rosenthal has indeed recorded that her committed acting and expressive presence, as much as her singing, contributed to her fame. By October she was singing the part of Lola in the first London performance of *Cavalleria Rusticana* at the Shaftesbury Theatre and she quickly made a successful operatic career. Her debut at Covent Garden came in 1893 in Gounod's *Faust*, the same year as she sang in the famous Cambridge University Musical Society Jubilee Concert subsequent to which Boito, Saint-Saëns, Bruch and Tchaikovsky received their honorary degrees. In 1894 Brema became the first British-born singer to be invited to Bayreuth, when Cosima Wagner summoned her for Ortrud in the first Bayreuth *Lohengrin* as well as for Kundry in *Parsifal*. George Bernard Shaw has left us a picture of this Bayreuth Ortrud:

Any less extraordinary person would have shattered herself with such dramatic violence as that with which she hurled herself into her invocation of Odin and the ancient gods: as it was the effect was less than she could have produced by simple singing without a movement. She rescued herself from the consequences of this resort to main force by still more main force, and finally came off as one of the most remarkable Ortruds we have seen, odious but frightfully strong. She sang with great power. One likes grit in an artist; but Miss Brema is all grit. I think she would be improved by being passed half a dozen times through a particularly heavy pair of millstones.

Earlier in the same year Shaw had observed:

When I first heard Miss Brema, I said 'it is magnificent but she will grind her voice to pieces in five years' ... In any reasonably artistic country Miss Brema would be pursuing a remarkable career on the lyric stage instead of wasting her qualities on the concert platform ... (her) performance entitles us to say in England that we have produced one of the very best living Wagnerian artists.

Henry Wood, too, described her as "a really great Wagner singer". Shaw, reporting a London performance in 1893, observed that:

Miss Maria Brema, who, happening to be tremendously in the dramatic vein, positively rampaged through Beethoven's Creation Hymn, scandalizing the Philharmonic, but carrying away the multitude.

And so we have this picture of her - exciting, dramatic, throwing caution to the winds, essentially 'operatic'. She returned to Bayreuth in 1896, when as Fricka she was the only English singer in *The Ring*, having meanwhile toured America with the Damrosch Opera Company singing in *Lohengrin, Tristan* and *Walküre*. In 1894/5 she had joined the Metropolitan Opera (New York) singing Amneris in *Aida* and Orpheus as well as her Wagner roles. In 1899 she was Paris's first Brangäne, singing in French, and in that year she was to sing the Narrator in Elgar's *Light of Life* at the Worcester Three Choirs Festival.

From the first there is evidence that Elgar had his doubts about Brema. On 7 July 1899 he wrote to Jaeger: "I see they have cast Marie Brema (!) for the little easy-going contralto part - I expect she will 'chuck it' - a festival committee is funny".

Whatever Elgar meant by 'chuck it', it does not sound like a compliment! In the event *The Times* recorded that "Mr. Elgar and his work were very warmly received", (Elgar conducted) and references to Brema were generally favourable - "a sympathetic exponent" according to *The Standard*. But a new, attractive young mezzo also made her Three Choirs debut in 1899, although the fee offered would apparently not cover the cost of her dress. Her name was Muriel Foster.

Muriel Foster, born in Sunderland on St. Cecilia's Day (22 November)

Muriel Foster

1877, was an extremely attractive 21 year old, still a student at the Royal College of Music where she had enrolled in 1896, singing in Verdi's *Falstaff* under Stanford in that year. In 1896 *Falstaff*'s Milan première was only three years past and Stanford had attended that performance and wrote a perceptive and detailed review for the *Daily Graphic*. Foster went on to make her professional debut in Parry's *King Saul* in Bradford (1896) and her London debut at the St. James's Popular Concerts with her twin sister Hilda, who retired on marriage. On 15 March 1900 Muriel sang Elgar's *Sea Pictures* at St. James's Hall and her teacher, Anna Williams, was moved to write to Elgar: "Let me tell you what a striking success my pupil Muriel Foster made at the Orchestral Concert of the RCM at St. James's Hall on the 15th in 4 of the songs from your *Sea Pictures. The Times* said she revealed beauties not hitherto brought out, and she and I have enjoyed working at them together".

It was of this performance that Stanford wrote to Elgar that Foster had not got "the whopping voice of C.B. (Clara Butt) but she has more poetry, and is musical to her finger tips". A week later Miss Williams was writing again to Elgar asking for some special composition from his pen for Foster on the occasion of the concert marking the Royal College's new hall: "I fancy she may be near Malvern soon, do if you possibly can hear her sing. She has a wonderful musical insight and imagination".

But in 1900 Elgar had other concerns than the encouragement of young unknowns. 1900 was the year of *Gerontius* and it was Brema who along with Edward Lloyd and Plunket Greene had been engaged to sing at the Birmingham première. It may be noted, however, that Winifred Ponder in her biography of Clara Butt (pp.187-8) contends that the part of the Angel was meant for Butt and "composed entirely with her voice in mind". Butt had, of course, triumphantly premièred *Sea Pictures* at the Norwich Festival on 5 October 1899. Winifred Ponder tells us that Butt assumed that the *Dream of Gerontius* première would also involve her, until she was disabused at a chance meeting with Brema "at tea after a Crystal Palace Concert". Brema told Butt that she was engaged to sing *The Dream of Gerontius* in Birmingham and asked Butt about her own Birmingham engagements. Miss Ponder's theory is that the Festival Committee wished to maximise commercial considerations - Butt would be a 'draw' in whatever she sang - in their programme arrangements.

In fact Brema came out of the disastrous affair reasonably well in comparison with the rest. Dora Penny claimed that she "saved the situation in Part II several times", and Willie Reed praised her "complete mastery and understanding". The *Manchester Guardian* found that "the grand style of Miss Brema was very finely exhibited", and the *Morning Leader* contended that "had the chorus, Dr. Richter and the other soloists understood their music as well as Miss Brema we should have had a perfect performance". But according to Rosa Burley, though only Brema "appeared to have any grasp of the emotions the music was supposed to express", even she, "a goddess from Valhalla if ever there was one, seemed unsuited for her part". And we have Vaughan Williams's famous recollection that "Greene had lost his voice - Miss Brema had none to lose". Certainly we know the devastating effect the failure had on Elgar, with his heart shut supposedly "against every religious feeling and every soft, gentle impulse for ever". Clearly he either did not blame the conductor, Hans Richter, or else he forgave him - for the other artists, I am not so sure.

In the summer of 1901 Marie Brema sang at Covent Garden in the brief run (two performances) of Stanford's *Much Ado About Nothing*, in which she was an "enchanting" Beatrice according to David Bispham, who sang opposite her. In 1902 she became Paris's first *Götterdämmerung* Brünnhilde, as in the case of *Gerontius*, under Richter's baton. Foster's great breakthrough came, of course, with the famous Düsseldorf *Gerontius* on 19 May 1902. This was the second of two great Düsseldorf performances - the second and third complete performances to be heard anywhere - which together totally rehabilitated the work. It is interesting to conjecture how it was that Foster, still only twenty-four years of age and at the outset of her career, came to be offered this overseas engagement. It may be significant that a year earlier, in February 1901, Elgar conducted Foster in *Sea Pictures* at a Bradford Concert which incidentally included an orchestral arrangement of the *Gerontius* 'Angel's Farewell'. Foster gave a "peculiarly artistic and sympathetic interpretation ... (and) thoroughly entered into the spirit of the music".

The first Düsseldorf *Gerontius* on 19 December 1901 had, for all its success, an inadequate Angel in Antonie Beel. With Foster's appearance the Angel's music was, in Michael Kennedy's words, "for the first time sung to true and beautiful effect". Henry Wood had never seen "an audience so excited nor a composer so spontaneously acclaimed" and, looking back later on Foster's career, surmised that Elgar had "conceived all his mezzo-soprano parts with Muriel Foster in mind. I do know that no other mezzo-soprano or contralto ever extracted a word of praise from him over their interpretation of his parts .. A richer, warmer mezzo-soprano voice I have rarely heard and her musicianship was of the highest".

Foster's triumph at Düsseldorf was in fact hard won. Her obituary notice in *The Times* refers to "agonies of nervousness" which she habitually suffered before she came on to the platform, and on this occasion she was additionally unwell and an apology was made on her behalf. "Miss Muriel Foster... though her voice was not in the best order owing to indisposition sang with beautiful tenderness", reported the *Daily Telegraph*. This was the performance which led to Richard Strauss's famous tribute to Elgar "the first English progressivist" and Foster never faltered in Elgar's affections from this point. After the Düsseldorf success, performances of *Gerontius* proliferated both in England and abroad. The Worcester Three Choirs Festival of 1902 saw Brema engaged but in the event, because of her indisposition, Foster singing the Angel once more. "Foster gave a rendering of the part of the Angel so rich in the noblest artistic qualities that she need not fear comparison with any rival", recorded the *Manchester Guardian* on 11 September - the very day that she signed Alice Elgar's autograph album. It may be seen at Elgar's Birthplace today! Elgar himself conducted as he did at the Secular Concert at which Foster sang three of the *Sea Pictures*.

Brema was still indisposed on 2 October when the work was repeated at Sheffield, and Foster again substituted, not only in *Gerontius* but also singing the première of the *Coronation Ode*, postponed because of the King's appendicitis from its originally projected London performance in June and now given in a gargantuan concert which also included the Prelude to Act III of *Lohengrin* and Beethoven's Violin Concerto with Wood conducting and Ysaÿe as soloist.

In March 1903 Brema and Foster sang the Angel on consecutive nights in two very interesting performances, Brema under Richter at Manchester on the 12th, "lending all the charm of her powerful and melodious voice to the performance" said the *Manchester Guardian*, and Foster on the 13th at Hanley with Elgar conducting the North Staffordshire Choral Society in a famous performance which I have described elsewhere (*Elgar Society Journal*, September 1981). It was this latter performance which convinced Elgar that this was the version which must be revived for the inevitable, first London performance already shamefully too-long delayed, and Lady Edmund Talbot, sister-in-law of the Duke of Norfolk, presented the opportunity with her notion of a performance at Westminster Cathedral. It is true that Elgar accepted, indeed welcomed, the substitution of Ludwig Wüllner, the hero of the Düsseldorf performance, for John Coates in the title role, but for the rest the Hanley performance ultimately transferred to London. But not without a certain amount of machination.

Immediately after her performance with Richter in Manchester, Brema was writing to Elgar (18 March 1903):

> I have had the great joy of once more taking part in your glorious work in Manchester - and am again singing the Angel on Tuesday in Liverpool - I wish

you were going to be there - are you? The Birmingham people have not written to me about the Festival. When I heard you were writing a work for it I, of course, hoped it would have a part for me in it. You had been pleased with my rendering of the Angel and I do hope ... you have not overlooked me in this new work of yours. I should feel it very sorely. Do let me hear soon whether there is any chance ... That we all rejoice that your great masterpiece is now appreciated everywhere I need not say.

The "new work" in which Brema hoped for a part was, of course, *The Apostles*, first performed in Birmingham on 14 October 1903. I have not come across Elgar's reply to this letter, but whereas Brema did not sing in *The Apostles* première, Muriel Foster did! Meanwhile, however, Brema duly sang her Liverpool *Gerontius* under Frederic Cowen, and with the esteemed Wüllner as Gerontius, on 24 March. Elgar was not present.

By now rumours of the forthcoming London *Gerontius* performance were rife. "It is a positive disgrace to London that it has not been heard there yet", wrote Thomas Dundas to Alice Elgar in early March, and added, interestingly, "Please give my regards to Dr. Elgar also, does he, I wonder, still smile at that old lady's remark about Miss Muriel Foster's 'pretty voice'?"; presumably in reference to some overheard conversation at Worcester the previous year.

On 22 March *The Sunday Special* reported that "Mr. Schulz-Curtius (a well known concert agent) has now definitely arranged with Dr. Richter and the Hallé executive ... we are to have the first performance of Dr. Elgar's Dream in London". The *Daily Telegraph* was still reporting such a project over a month later (29 April). But in fact for one thing Forsyth, secretary of the Hallé Concerts Society, had written to Elgar on 27 March to the effect that no such performance could be brought about before October - "The orchestra is now dispersed" - and, in any case, Elgar, as we know, from mid-March onwards was committed totally to the North Staffordshire Choral Society and, as it transpired, Foster!

But it was the rumoured Hallé performance of which Brema got wind. She wrote to Elgar on the subject in a letter, the date of which is not entirely clear because of Brema's eccentric calligraphy, but is probably 18 April. She was "greatly distressed to hear nothing about the Angel. It would be extremely hard on me if I were to be left out, considering I first sang the part and - as you told me - to your satisfaction and pleasure ... I have lately proved to people that my severe illness has not got in any way impaired my voice which in fact has never been better than now ... I had hopes you would not allow me to be forgotten". This was the letter which produced Elgar's well known reply of 24 April.

Dear Madame Brema,
    I am sorry you have had no reply. We only returned from the North late last night. I have, of course, in memory your fine and intellectual creation of the part; and, although I never thought the 'tessitura' suited you well, as the magnificent artist you are, you made it go very finely. I do not know anything of the Schulz-Curtius performance. If it is a repitition (sic) of the Manchester performance I have no doubt the authorities will apply to you. Very many thanks for all your Paris news, and with our very kind regards,

Believe me
Yours sincerely
Edward Elgar

In fact the letter ("a tactful evasion rather than a heart-felt compliment", Michael Kennedy calls it) takes a lot of believing. As I have indicated Elgar knew plenty about the Schulz-Curtius projected performance and, indeed, that it had foundered. He knew that the London première was arranged for 6 June, that the North Staffordshire Choral Society was to sing it, that he himself was to conduct it, and that, after a struggle, he had got his own way regarding Foster's singing the Angel! None of this he vouchsafes to Brema!
    Indeed Foster, too, had written to Elgar on the subject in an undated letter, but arriving before Brema's.

Dear Dr. Elgar,
    I have heard that there is a possibility of Gerontius being done in London. I am writing to ask you to put in a good word for me. I love the part so much and would very much like to sing it in London.

She need not have worried. Elgar put in more than a good word, he entered into a battle with the impressario and erstwhile secretary to Paderewski, Hugo Görlitz, who was organising matters with Westminster Cathedral, and brooked no contradiction on the point.
    On 31 March, Görlitz wrote to Elgar:

With regard to the soloists I shall be only too pleased to be guided by your decision and wishes, but unfortunately as regards the contralto, I have my own contralto to whom I am bound by contract to give the first chance. Of course, I have gone into the matter thoroughly, and if my contralto falls short of requirements when you hear her, I am quite willing to ask Miss Foster, but I am afraid Miss Foster will not give her services, and I shall not employ anybody who does not give their services for such an occasion.

The performance was to be for Cathedral Charities.
Elgar replied by return, for by 2 April Görlitz was writing once more:

> I am very pleased to have your letter of yesterday's date, and I shall be guided by your wishes in every respect where it is feasible. I want, however, to ask one question. If Miss Foster is not obtainable, may I offer the engagement to Miss Brema?

No mention of this suggestion in Elgar's letter to Brema three weeks later! By 14 April, however, Görlitz was able to indicate to Elgar that a telegram from St. Petersburg confirmed Miss Foster's availability.

Görlitz surrendered but with ill grace. On 29 April he was writing to Elgar:

> I think I ought to make quite clear to you the position in which I am standing towards the performance of The Dream of Gerontius. The Administrator of the Cathedral would not allow the use of it until I guaranteed the expenses. These will amount to over £1,000. This was also the reason why I should like to have put in artists of my own choice, who would have done the work equal justice to those engaged, and I could have supplied them free of charge. Although I do not object to any suggestion made, it is rather an unusual thing that an artist who will not even engage herself except through her own agent has to appear at a concert of which I am undertaking to pay the losses, if any.

And on 14 May:

> Dr. Wüllner will not attend the rehearsal on Saturday morning, and it will be just as well if I have a substitute for Miss Foster on the Friday. In fact I think you owe me that, for I want to convince you that there are other artists who can sing the music quite as well as Miss Foster.

Clearly Görlitz had some knowledge of Foster's proposed movements because she did in fact write to Alice Elgar on 19 May: "Perhaps it would not put Dr. Elgar out very much if I only attended part of Friday's rehearsal as, of course, I do not want to give up my concert".

Permission was readily granted: "It is very good of you to let me off part of Friday's rehearsal", wrote Foster three days later to Elgar, "Thank you ever so much for the charming photo which I am proud to have ... it is an excellent likeness".

Foster could do no wrong! Four months after the Westminster *Gerontius*, in which Foster at least received unanimous acclaim, Jaeger was writing to Elgar (23 October) : "How is Muriel the gorgeous?"

It must have been the final straw for Görlitz to read in the course of a wildly inaccurate review in *The Tablet*: "We cannot but congratulate Mr. Görlitz on his excellent judgement in choosing so admirable an exponent of the part".

Though Brema sang in the next London performance of *Gerontius* on 15 February 1904 - Jaeger reporting to Elgar that it was an "uninspiring performance" in which Brema "rubatoed dreadfully & threw poor Conductor Fagge & orchestra out" - her career as an Elgarian was largely over.

Jaeger appears to have been among those who by this time felt that Brema, now approaching 50, had seen better days. In a letter to Sidney Loeb dated 31 October 1904 he writes: "I prefer the handsome Muriel as the 'Angel' in our friends Gerontius. I used to admire Mme Brema greatly, but even an idolator like unto ye cant affirm upon oath that her voice & method are like unto what they used to be".

Brema was passed over for both *Gerontius* and *The Apostles* at the great Covent Garden Elgar Festival in March 1904. Muriel Foster was not available because of engagements in America and H.V. Higgins, Chairman of the Covent Garden Opera Syndicate, wrote to Elgar on 19 December 1903: "I had naturally thought of Brema but I am told on the very best authority that on the last two or three occasions which she sang it was almost painful ... I cannot help feeling that no amount of poetic feeling will compensate for a raucous voice".

And again ten days later (29 December):

> My Dear Elgar,
>   Many thanks for your letter. I have told Schulz-Curtius to communicate with Lunn as regards The Apostles and with Butt as regards Gerontius. Rightly or wrongly, I think that Butt's voice will more than compensate for her lack of intelligence and that on the whole the public will prefer her to Brema.

When Butt's terms proved "prohibitive", Higgins asked Elgar in a letter of 9 January whether he preferred Brema for *Gerontius* or Lunn to sing both. It was the latter solution which carried the day and Kirkby Lunn sang both works on the consecutive nights of 14 and 15 March.

However, Brema's career continued to be significant. In 1904, in complaining disbelievingly at her and David Bispham's omission from the Leeds Festival, Stanford conjectured that it must be for reasons of "economy": "It cannot be that they are not good enough, for they are two of the biggest artists we have anywhere".

She continued to sing in works such as *Tristan* and *Lohengrin* at Covent Garden until 1907. In 1910 she organised the first of three seasons of opera in

English at the Savoy, singing Orpheus in her own production. "How she trained that chorus to get their words over the footlights as they did is a secret I have never been able to unravel", recalled Henry Wood. In 1913 she was appointed to the Chief Professorship of Singing at the Royal Manchester College of Music at an annual salary of £400 per annum plus a weekly first class return railway ticket to London. She also took charge of the opera class at £20 per term. She was, writes Michael Kennedy in his history of the College, "the most dynamic personality" among the singing teachers. Her "principal virtue was her ability to infuse dullards with life even if the effects were sometimes unduly, even grotesquely exaggerated".

She was involved in controversy with the inimitable Beecham when in December 1914 he was invited to address the College Annual Meeting and used the opportunity to launch a typical broadside. The College, he said, was only 21 years' old. If it were one of the "old established perfectly useless institutions like those in London", he would not have troubled to say a word about it. He never troubled to listen to singers who applied to him from the London Colleges, "especially that great bazaar the Guildhall School", because he knew they would be bad. "But you are young and enthusiastic and though you have up to the present time accomplished absolutely nothing there is still plenty of time, and you will probably not make the same mistakes as your hopelessly effete, played out and useless brethren in London. I don't know", he continued, "how many students are studying singing in this College, very few I hope!" The condition of English singing was "hopeless" and "tragic".

Correspondents to the *Manchester Guardian* were not slow to defend the College and one letter from the Acting-Principal, Stanley Withers, instanced Brema's recent student production of Purcell's *Dido* (July 1914). Beecham returned with a specific onslaught directed against *Dido* and Brema. *Dido* was "a work performed in Europe perhaps once in 100 years and of a character entirely different as regards style and stage movements to anything else they may ever be called upon in the future to take part in". A year had been wasted on " this archaic piece ... to gain for the College a reputation for exoticism and antiquarianism in taste, to exploit the fad of a celebrated artist and to obtain a laudatory notice in a certain London newspaper (*The Times*) which ... has always been the sturdy champion of musical reaction in England". Brema was moved to grant a press interview to defend her position and the controversy, largely tongue-in-cheek on Beecham's part, died down.

Brema died in harness in March 1925, being taken ill on one of her regular visits to the College. Prior to this, though, there was one latter-day connection with Elgar. She had married a Liverpool businessman, Arthur Brand, and her daughter Tita Brand in turn married the Belgian poet Emile Cammaerts.

When Elgar set Cammaerts's poem *Après Anvers* as *Carillon* during the First World War, it was Tita Brand who recited its première at the Queen's Hall on 7 December 1914. Tita Brand inherited the Wagnerian qualities which, I suspect, somewhat put Elgar off Brema. The daughter was, recalls Henry Wood, "an enormous woman with a deep speaking voice", and he recounts that when she had solicited George Bernard Shaw for a part in one of his plays, he had replied:

> Dear Miss Brand,
>   Many thanks for your little note. I am one of the greatest admirers of your art, but I should not dream of employing a London and North Western railway engine to draw a baby carriage. Love to your mother.

A brush off, one feels, somewhat more direct than Elgar's evasions towards the mother in 1903!

Rosa Burley was at the *Carillon* première and recalled that, Mme Brand-Cammaerts being pregnant, an enormous bank of roses was built on the platform to conceal the fact. Over this the artist "appeared rather in the manner of a Punch and Judy show". Notwithstanding her condition, Brand put such energy into her performance that, Rosa Burley goes on, "both Edward and I trembled for the effect on her".

Meanwhile Foster's close connection with Elgar deepened. She duly sang in *The Apostles* première in Birmingham on 14 October 1903. "If we must differentiate ... we are inclined to place in the front Miss Muriel Foster", reported *The Times*. In 1905 she was one of a handful of singers, not including Brema, whom Elgar exempted from a Beecham-type attack on the quality of English singing in one of his Birmingham lectures. In that year, too, she married Ludovic Goetz (who became a director of the Royal Academy of Music) and for a while, because of this and a loss of voice through illness, her appearances became intermittent. Subsequently, of course, she did recover with, it is said, even greater interpretive power, singing in the première of *The Kingdom* on 3 October 1906, and emerging from retirement to take part in the Jaeger Memorial Concert on 24 January 1910 and the première of *The Music Makers* on 1 October 1912. In 1914 she was awarded the Gold Medal of the Philharmonic Society, an award for which Elgar himself had to wait until 1925.

Socially as well as professionally, Foster's links with Elgar increased. They were frequent visitors to one anothers' homes. We read that it was at the Goetzes that Elgar met Paderewski in June 1911 while, when the Elgars moved to Severn House, Hampstead in the same year, the Goetzes presented them with a settee. Percy Young tells of Elgar and Muriel Foster motoring over to Broadheath from the 1912 Hereford Three Choirs, and she was among the guests at the first, private, performance of the Violin Sonata at Severn House on 15 October 1918. Later in the same month we read of Elgar and Foster, the one on the cymbals, the other along with Myra Hess as a nightingale, taking part in a Queen's Hall performance of *The Toy Symphony* in aid of the Red Cross.

Percy Young, too, in *Elgar O.M.* tells of Muriel Foster's influence in reviving Elgar's interest in a Cello Concerto. He writes that an amateur cellist called Thomas More, a former pupil of Casals and a friend of Foster, was staying with the Goetzes and expressed surprise that Elgar had never composed a concerto for cello. Without more ado Foster wrote to Edward on this subject and within a week had a reply to the effect that More's interest had revived Elgar's own in some old sketches on which he would set to work. More subsequently attended the première of the Cello Concerto at Elgar's invitation but, so the story goes, did not meet the composer because the performance was so bad that he felt inhibited from speaking to Elgar about it.

Muriel Foster's close friendship with the Elgars continued right down to Alice's death. Alice's diary records her ringing on 11 November 1918, as Edward was hoisting a "gorgeous" flag to celebrate the Armistice in the war which had moved Ludovic Goetz to change his name by deed poll to that of his wife's maiden name, while on 25 March 1920, Muriel was the last person outside the family to visit the dying Alice. In a letter to Alice Stuart Wortley shortly after his wife's death, Elgar referred to the affectionate familiarity of Alice and Muriel: "she always called Alice 'the Little Wren'." Thereafter the connection was more tenuous as Elgar withdrew from so many past associations and Foster's professional career was largely over. She and her husband both contributed five guineas to the Broadheath Birthplace Appeal after Elgar's death. She died in London on 23 December 1937.

It is, perhaps, strange that Elgar never dedicated a work to Muriel Foster. His *Carissima* for small orchestra of 1913 was in fact dedicated to her sister Winifred Stephens, while his song *A Child Asleep* written in 1909 is dedicated to her son Anthony Goetz. (There is a familiar photograph of Elgar with Anthony Goetz taken in about 1915 at Severn House.) Michael Kennedy lists a projected scena *Callicles* with a text by Matthew Arnold as being for Muriel Foster. Elgar worked on sketches in 1913 but it was never completed. Foster certainly on occasion pleaded for a piece from Elgar, as in this letter probably written in 1903:

> Do you think you will be likely to feel like writing a scena for me some time this winter? I would be more than proud and grateful if you would. I go to America early next year and want one so badly. Forgive my boldness in asking.

But, as I have said, Henry Wood believed that Elgar wrote all his mezzo parts after 1902 with her in mind. Ernest Newman considered that no one could surpass her as the Angel, and for Gervase Elwes she was "the best Angel of all". Elgar himself greeted Foster at the 1909 Birmingham Festival, at a time when she had retired from the concert platform following her marriage, with the gift of a page from his sketchbook which he inscribed:

> First sketch for Intro: to Section IV of 'The Kingdom' which section was written for Mrs Goetz & was, apparently, not good enough for her as she sings it no more!
>
> Leaving
Edward Elgar
to his fate
(which is sad)

And that is about all I have to say about Marie Brema and Muriel Foster. As far as I am aware neither has had a biographer and neither has left us a recording. How marvellous it would be to hear them! They were central characters in the period of Elgar's greatest accomplishment and their association with *Gerontius*, especially, will assure their immortality. If, as far as Elgar was concerned there was a 'winner' and that 'winner' was Foster, then Brema had her other dual career as Wagnerian operatic star and Professor at the Manchester College to sustain her co-equal claim to the public's, if not Elgar's, affections.

BIBLIOGRAPHY

Allen, Kevin: *August Jaeger : Portrait of Nimrod* (Ashgate 2000)
Boden, Anthony: *Three Choirs. A History of the Festival* (Alan Sutton 1992)
Burley, Rosa & Carruthers, Frank C: *Edward Elgar : The Record of a Friendship* (Barrie & Jenkins 1972)
Elkins, Robert: *Queen's Hall, 1893-1941* (Rider & Co., London 1944)
Elwes, Winifride & Elwes, Richard: *Gervase Elwes* (Grayson & Grayson, London 1935)
Fifield, Christopher: *True Artist and True Friend : A Biography of Hans Richter* (Oxford University Press, 1993)
Greene, H. Plunket: *Charles Villiers Stanford* (Edward Arnold, London 1935)
Hodgkins, Geoffrey (Ed): *The Best of Me : A Gerontius Centenary Companion* (Elgar Editions 1999)
Kennedy, Michael: *Portrait of Elgar* (2nd Edition Oxford University Press, 1982)
Kennedy, Michael: *The Hallé Tradition* (Manchester University Press, 1960)

Kennedy, Michael: *The History of the Royal Manchester College of Music* (Manchester University Press, 1971)

Kennedy, Michael: *The Works of Ralph Vaughan Williams* (Oxford University Press, 1964)

Moore, Jerrold Northrop: *Edward Elgar : A Creative Life* (Oxford University Press, 1984)

Moore, Jerrold Northrop: *Elgar and His Publishers : Letters of a Creative Life* (Oxford University Press, 1987)

Moore, Jerrold Northrop: *Edward Elgar : Letters of a Lifetime* (Oxford University Press, 1990)

Norris, Gerald: *Stanford, the Cambridge Jubilee and Tchaikovsky* (David & Charles, 1980)

Ponder, Winifred: *Clara Butt : Her Life Story* (Harrap & Co., London, 1928)

Powell, Mrs Richard C: *Edward Elgar : Memories of a Variation* (Remploy Reprint, London 1979)

Reed, W.H: *Elgar* (J.M. Dent & Son, London 1939)

Rosenthal, Harold: *Two Centuries of Opera at Covent Garden* (Putnam, London 1958)

Shaw, H. Watkins: *The Three Choirs Festival* (Ebeneezer Baylis & Son, London 1954)

Wood, Sir Henry J: *My Life of Music* (Victor Gollancz, London 1938)

Young, Percy M: *Elgar O.M.* (White Lion Publishers, London 1973)

Young, Percy M: *A Future For English Music : and Other Lectures by Edward Elgar* (Dennis Dobson, London 1968)

Young, Percy M: *Alice Elgar : Enigma of a Victorian Lady* (Dennis Dobson, London 1978)

Young, Percy M: *Letters to Nimrod from Edward Elgar* (Dennis Dobson, London 1965)

Young, Percy M: *Letters of Edward Elgar* (Geoffrey Bles, London 1956)

The writings of G.B. Shaw are to be found in *Shaw's Music : The Bodley Head G.B.S.*

The cuttings book at the Elgar Birthplace, Lower Broadheath, is a mine of information gleaned from contemporary newspapers.

Letters from Edward Elgar, Anna Williams, Marie Brema, Thomas Dundas, Muriel Foster, Hugo Görlitz, A.J. Jaeger, H.V. Higgins are contained in the Elgar Archive at the Worcester Public Records Office.

CONDUCTOR:
Mr. J. WHEWALL.

*James Whewall, with some of the competition medals won by the
North Staffordshire Chorus and its forerunners under his direction*

ELGAR AND THE POTTERIES CHOIR MASTER

In October 1902 Elgar received a letter from William Sherratt, organist to the North Staffordshire and District Choral Society, extending an invitation to conduct *Gerontius* in Hanley. The driving forces behind this suggestion were in fact Havergal Brian, then a youthful admirer of Elgar and rising local musician, and Arthur Bailey, treasurer of the Choir, Sherratt proving useful no doubt as original point of contact in view of his having been organist at Elgar's last appearance in the Potteries for the première in 1896 of *King Olaf*. A meeting was quickly arranged and a delegation waited upon Elgar in Malvern. The composer was offered his choice of soloists and orchestra, and convinced of the ability of the Choir by reference to competitive successes. By 13 October Sherratt was writing to Alice Elgar to express his "gratification" at Elgar's agreement to conduct. It was the beginning of an exciting period of association between the composer and the Choir, and the introduction to Elgar of its remarkable Chorus Master, the taciturn James Whewall who had sat anonymously in a corner at the Craeg Lea discussions. "Might I ask who is the gentleman to be responsible for the Choir?" Elgar had asked at length. Arthur Bailey pointed to the small, neat, unlikely figure of Whewall.

Havergal Brian has recalled Whewall as "the greatest enigma I ever met. He baffled every man who met him for the first time. He had nothing to say, speech was of no use to him - his genius was essentially musical. He never evinced any enthusiasm for literature or the other arts ... even in conversation on music he didn't enthuse", and Brian goes on to confirm that "on deputations to composers, conductors, etc ... on each occasion I had to transpose his thoughts into speech". But of his musical genius there was no doubt. "When he faced a choir his silence was broken. Here the real man stood revealed ... the quiet man gave way to one of astonishing energy and vigour".

Whewall was born at Kingsley, near Leek, and as a boy sang in the Choir of the Parish Church. Subsequently he became Choir Master at a Wesleyan Chapel and organiser of a local juvenile chorus with which he obtained his first competitive successes. Out of this chorus developed, as the members matured, the Talke and District Choir which in 1900 tied for first prize in the Small Choir section of the Welsh National Eisteddfod.

By profession, Whewall had been a coal miner, but a serious accident caused him to leave the pit and to concentrate virtually all his energies on the

Choir. His new occupation of insurance collector was almost deliberately geared to assisting him in maintaining contacts with his singers, while it has been suggested by Reginald Nettel, in his *North Staffordshire Music*, he asserted his primacy the more through his music in order to convince himself that he was not a coward. In rehearsals his motto was "thorough". "No conductor could be more determined to make tell every moment given to rehearsal, and few got through more work in a short time", observed the *Staffordshire Sentinel* in 1909. "When you went to rehearsal under James Whewall, you went to work", recalled one Choir member. The best remembered story of his discipline is his ban on the wearing of corsets among choristers since this he believed was prejudicial to good breath control! By the time of the approach to Elgar, the Choir had been enlarged, the name of the North Staffordshire and District Choral Society adopted and the unique triumph of carrying off the main National Eisteddfod class in consecutive years (1901 at Merthyr Tydfil and 1902 at Bangor) achieved.

The Hanley performance of *Gerontius* duly took place on 13 March 1903 and was a huge success. Even the less than ideal expedient of merging a contingent of the Hallé Orchestra with a group of local players proved quite satisfactory, while the meticulous preparation of the chorus (Whewall even insisting that Elgar mark the score at points where the choir should stand so that he might "drill them") and the distinguished soloists (John Coates, David Ffrangcon Davies, Muriel Foster) ensured a triumph. Alice Elgar, writing to Dora Penny, soon sets aside the "horrid journey" and extols the "splendid chorus rehearsal ... so fresh and spontaneous ... E had no trouble and they took all his nuances at once". As for the performance itself, "First came Froissart beautifully played, then Sea Pictures (3), and two choruses, and then a reception in the Mayor's Parlour ... then a most beautiful performance of Gerontius. I think I never heard anything more lovely than the beginning of the Kyrie and so it went on, simply splendid and such enthusiasm".

After the performance Elgar was apparently too overcome with emotion to say anything but the *Staffordshire Sentinel* predicted that "there will be no room for surprise if he does not candidly admit that it was the best reading of the Dream that he had yet heard". And indeed Elgar subsequently wrote to Frederick Meier, the Secretary of the Choir: "I was delighted, and, I will add, deeply impressed by their performance. I have rarely heard such finished, musicianly singing, and have never had less trouble to get my exact reading ... This was made easy for me by the splendid training of Mr. Whewall ... The tone is magnificent - silvery, yet solid, well-balanced and sonorous, and the attack fine. I place the Chorus in the highest rank, and I thank the members for giving me the opportunity of hearing a performance of my work almost flawless". To the bass soloist, Ffrangcon Davies, he contented himself with the more modest observation: "I am told the work made an effect and my dear wife seems beaming with happiness". The performance was further commemorated by the presentation to Elgar of the Gerontius Cup, a piece standing 12 inches in height made by C.J. Nokes at the Doulton Factory, which today is to be seen at the Birthplace.

The clearest evidence that Elgar had indeed meant what he wrote is that within two days of the performance he was suggesting the Chorus for the projected London première of *Gerontius* in Westminster Cathedral. The enthusiasm of the chorus can be gauged by the fact that, before March was out, Meier was writing to Elgar making the identical suggestion on the supposed basis of reading a newspaper rumour of a proposed performance by "the Hallé people". There was no need to await any such development argued Meier - "our people are ready and willing ... and they would be prepared to pay their own travelling expenses. Can't this be arranged soon?" Whewall was even prepared to abandon his ambition of a third Eisteddfod triumph in favour of the project. On 4 April Jaeger wrote to Elgar of a visit of the Hanley Committee to London to negotiate details with the impresario Hugo Görlitz and their clear preference that Elgar, not Richard Strauss or Mengelberg, should conduct: "they want you to conduct 'cos they are proud of you, I daresay", a preference which subsequently led to the withdrawal of the Amsterdam Orchestra from the performance.

The Westminster *Gerontius* was a highlight in the association of Elgar and the North Staffordshire Choir. Whewall carried out his usual meticulous preparation, including a public open rehearsal on 25 May in Hanley. At 3.30am on Saturday 6 June, the day of the performance, a special train began its tour of the Potteries Halts picking up the Choir. It was a dull, cold morning and the train ran an hour late. After breakfasting hastily at the St. James's Restaurant, Piccadilly, the Choir was whisked by omnibuses to a rehearsal at the Cathedral scheduled for 9am but now unavoidably late. Elgar placed Whewall at his side and found few problems with the singing apart from the difficulty of registering a piano effect in the vast, unfinished building. The rehearsal, however, was protracted since the makeshift orchestra was "frequently called to book for sins of omission and commission". There was just time for a rushed lunch before the performance started at 3pm.

On the face of it the Choir triumphed once again. All tickets had been sold, and the vast, fashionable audience made the London *Gerontius* the great musical event of the year. Whewall felt that he had never before been so moved by the rendering of a musical composition. While the Elgars departed with the Schusters to the Hut at Bray, the Choir was feted by Görlitz back at

WESTMINSTER CATHEDRAL

AMBROSDEN AVENUE, VICTORIA STREET, S.W.

(By Gracious Permission of H.E. Cardinal Vaughan).

Saturday Afternoon, June 6, 1903, at 3.

FIRST PERFORMANCE IN LONDON

OF

The Dream of Gerontius

(EDWARD ELGAR)

Under the Sole Management of Mr. HUGO GÖRLITZ
(119, New Bond Street, London. W.).

Tenor - - - Dr. LUDWIG WÜLLNER

Mezzo-Soprano - Miss MURIEL FOSTER

Bass - - - Mr. FFRANGCON DAVIES

AND

Chorus of the North Staffordshire District Choral Society

(Conductor—Mr. J. WHEWALL)

FULL ORCHESTRA

Conductor - Dr. EDWARD ELGAR.

Organist – Mr. R. R. TERRY.

The net proceeds will be for the Benefit of the Cathedral Choir Schools.

PRICE ONE SHILLING.

NOVELLO AND COMPANY LIMITED, PRINTERS LONDON.

Cover of the programme for the first London performance of
The Dream of Gerontius

the St. James's Restaurant. In a humorous speech he attributed the success of the Choir to Potteries Beer (or ginger beer - remembering, perhaps, the large Methodist contingent) as opposed to whisky. The National Anthem was sung and *For He's a Jolly Good Fellow* rendered in tribute to Whewall "with such heartiness that the room seemed to vibrate in apparent sympathy", observed R.W.Ship, musical correspondent of the *Staffordshire Sentinel.* The taciturn Whewall was moved to reply. It was, he said, "the proudest moment of my life".

By Monday, however, it was clear that the Choir shared to an extent the mixed critical reception which greeted the performance. For the *Daily Mail* they "sang wonderfully well" and according to the *Daily Chronicle* "made a great impression", but *The Standard* noted that "effects were not always satisfactory" and the *Monthly Musical Review* condemned their performance as "tame and colourless". Both the *Staffordshire Sentinel* and Elgar were incensed. The composer wrote to thank the Choir for "their splendid performance in London", while the local newspaper observed that "something would have appeared to have gone wrong with the London press" and took the critics to task for their niggardly and ungracious response, speculating that journalists did not perhaps care to be called out on a Saturday afternoon and, more pertinently, commenting on the "inexplicable" misjudgement of seating critics "behind pillars and masses of masonry" which obstructed both sight and sound.

However, immediately after this perfomance (11 June) Meier was writing to Elgar to re-open a matter already raised back in March, namely "producing in this district your new work The Apostles under exactly the same conditions as our recent performance". *The Apostles*, with Elgar again conducting, was given in Hanley but not until 30 March 1905 and not before Meier ("smart, business-like and pushful", according to R.W.Ship) had experience of how elusive Elgar could be.

First Elgar was unsure whether he would be in England in March 1904, nor was he to be pinned down to a date in April or May. Without the composer, the undertaking "would, without doubt, be a failure", argued Meier. A clear assurance was needed before commitment to such "heavy financial liability". The project was deferred until November 1904 and instead Sullivan's *Light of the World* mounted in the spring. In April 1904 Meier, armed with favourable reviews of the Sullivan, was still trying to pin Elgar down, and in June he nearly lost him! "Your decision if unaltered means a death blow to our Society ... The public expect and are looking forward to your visit ... we dare not come before the public, after repeated announcements, unless the work be The Apostles under the composer's personal direction. We are as yet in our infancy as a Choral Society and have an uphill fight against prejudice in this district". Despite this desperate plea the November arrangements also fell through. But at least Meier got a more definite assurance from Elgar about the following spring, and Whewall obtained consolation by returning to Wales for a further Eisteddfod victory at Rhyl. Subsequent negotiations went more smoothly apart from Elgar's refusal to fall in with the suggestion of "giving a chance" to a local singer in the part of Peter. Though an interesting late replacement among the soloists was Gervase Elwes, "little known locally" but "secured on the nomination of Sir Edward Elgar" when the tenor Evan Williams went down with laryngitis. He joined such well-tried Elgarians as Muriel Foster, Ffrangcon Davies and Andrew Black while, as in 1903, the Hallé provided the band.

At the final rehearsal, closed because of the numbers seeking admission, Elgar met with his usual "great reception". He was, he announced, "not quite well" and proposed to make a light evening of it. But by the end the excellence of Whewall's preparation had quite perked him up, while among the few admitted to the hall was Henry Wood (whose wife was also among the soloists) who insisted on adding his impromptu congratulations on "the exceptionally fine singing." The performance was another great triumph: "A Great Evening" proclaimed the *Sentinel*'s headline. The audience was of capacity. A bouquet of orchids from the ladies of the Choir awaited Alice in her seat.

The gentlemen, not withstanding their working class status, were "without exception in evening costume", the ladies in uniform cream dress. "It may be said without exaggeration", commented the *Sentinel* "that the singing of the Choir was the finest which has yet been heard in the work". As for Elgar, "even as a conductor there is something about the man which places him on the mountain tops". Alice was "so stirred ... that with moist eyes and quivering voice she said she thought it impossible that the work could be done at any time better than it had been done that night". Wood thought it "wonderful" and expressed the wish to hear the performance transferred to London. Whewall was elated at the ovation which greeted him at the conclusion. "This", said Elgar, "is the gentleman responsible for it all".

In his customary letter of thanks, Elgar called the performance "superb", and went on to say that "so far as my experience goes (the choruses) have never been sung with more intelligence, pathos and force ... I have been, as you know, very unwell for more than a month and have had to give up many engagements, and, somewhat against my doctor's wishes I made a special effort to be with you and was amply repaid". All the long negotiations and machinations were forgotten.

In 1906 Whewall, though having no liking nor aptitude for orchestral conducting, gave a performance of *Gerontius* in Hanley, resulting, recalled R.W.Ship, in "a very fine entertainment". Later in the same year the Choir was yet again placed first at the Caernavon Eisteddfod. Meanwhile Elgar was completing his new oratorio *The Kingdom*, which was to have its first performance at Birmingham on 3 October. A year later, Tuesday 15 October 1907, Elgar returned to Hanley with this latest choral masterpiece. Inevitably there was the familiar "rousing reception" at rehearsal, and a capacity audience which included the Grand Duke Michael of Russia. The performance was judged to be "not a flawless representation, but ... as near being perfect as is likely to be reached for some time to come". Shortage of rehearsal time explained any shortcoming, but the *Sentinel* could not resist a comparison with the Leeds Festival performance of the previous Friday; the Staffordshire Choir "succeeded where the Yorkshire singers failed". Of the original Birmingham soloists, John Coates was joined by Frederic Austin, Mrs Henry Wood and Miss Grainger Kerr. The Birmingham Symphony Orchestra, having been passed over in favour of the Hallé at the première in its native city, now provided the band. At the close Elgar "was recalled three times, and the Chorus would not leave their seats until the trainer had received the ovation to which they knew he was justly entitled". It was another joint triumph for Elgar and Whewall, but there were to be no more oratorios and this was to be their last appearance together.

Whewall was to have further success, such as the London performance of Delius's *Sea Drift* in February 1909 and the *Mass of Life* in June of the same year, both under Beecham. But the final recognition, which to an extent involved Elgar once more, was the Command Performance at Windsor to which the Choir was summoned on 15 October 1909. The occasion was the visit of King Manuel of Portugal who, together with Edward VII and the Queen, the Queen of Norway, the Prince and Princess of Wales, Asquith and Grey, were among the glittering audience. The Choir did not leave the Potteries until mid-afternoon and within a few minutes of their arrival were required to take their positions in St. George's Hall. But Whewall later observed that all went off "without a hitch", and that Elgar's song *Weary Wind of the West* made the greatest impression on the King, who "applauded vigorously at its conclusion". Dr W.G.McNaught, later editor of *The Musical Times* but now a close supporter of the Choir, described this rendition as "gorgeous", while the performance of another Elgar piece, *Go Song of Mine* was "very fine". It was one of the "red letter days" of his life. At the conclusion the King approached Whewall and offered congratulations, observing that he had never heard such singing in his life; and indeed he had demanded a number of encores including Barnby's *Sweet and Low*. Queen Alexandra presented a box of chocolates to each member of the choir.

Still the day was not at an end. At Windsor Railway Station, the Choir sang two pieces for the benefit of the vast crowd of townsfolk assembled. Whewall had made two visits to Windsor and two to Buckingham Palace to see to arrangements, and had been dashing to and fro to Wales as an Eisteddfod adjudicator. He was 58 years old and as some of the men hoisted him shoulder high to conduct on the station platform, it was reported that they "noticed the deadly pallor of his face in the lamp-light".

On the 19th Whewall's illness was announced and he was unable to rehearse the Choir, "an almost unheard of abstention". The Whewall Benefit Concert, arranged in Hanley for the 25th, in the form of a repeat of the Windsor programme, was taken over by McNaught. "The Choir", said the *Sentinel* "sang as if inspired". The programme included, as an encore, the ladies singing 'In Haven' from *Sea Pictures*. Two days later Whewall underwent an operation for appendicitis, apparently successfully, but subsequently there were complications and he died on the evening of 28 November. According to Arthur Bailey, who had succeeded Meier as Choir Secretary, his last message was: "Remember me to all members of my dear Choir; I love them, and I know they all love me".

Vast crowds attended the funeral at which the Choir sang *Jesu Lover of My Soul* at the graveside. A letter of sympathy was received from the King and Queen, hard upon one which had followed the news of his illness. Doggerel verse was contributed in considerable quantity to the *Sentinel*:

> Weep England, weep for now he moves no more
> His baton free to sway the glorious song,
> Which swells from earth to open heaven's door,
> And moves the pulse of all the listening throng!

began one such offering.

From Hereford came a telegram to the widow: "Deeply grieved to hear of loss of your husband whom I valued and admired greatly. My sincerest sympathy with you and the Choral Society. Edward Elgar".

It was the end of an episode in Elgar's career and in Potteries music.

A contemporary Potteries scene - Longton in c1910

BIBLIOGRAPHY

Ffrangcon-Davies, Marjorie: *David Frangcon-Davies : His Life and Book* (John Lane, The Bodley Head, 1938)

MacDonald, Malcolm: *Havergal Brian : Music : Vol 1 British Music* (Toccata Press, 1986)

Moore, Jerrold Northrop: *Edward Elgar : A Creative Life* (Oxford University Press, 1984)

Moore, Jerrold Northrop: *Elgar and His Publishers : Letters of a Creative Life* (Oxford University Press, 1987)

Nettel, R: *Music in the Five Towns : 1840-1914* (Oxford University Press, 1944)

Nettel, R: *Ordeal By Music* (Oxford University Press, 1945)

Nettel, R: *North Staffordshire Music : A Social Experiment* (Triad Press, 1977)

Ship, R.W: *A History of the North Staffordshire and District Choral Society* (Hanley 1909)

Letters of William Sherratt and Frederick Meier are contained in the Elgar Collection at the Worcester Public Records Office.

A main source for any study of the North Staffordshire and District Choral Society are the files of the *Staffordshire Sentinel* which may be consulted at the Hanley Central Library, to whose staff I am indebted. I am also grateful to the Librarian of the *Staffordshire Sentinel* (Mrs B.Mansfeld when I was first researching this topic) at Northcliffe House, Hanley, Stoke-on-Tent.

Cuttings from numerous national newspapers are retained in the cuttings books at the Elgar Birthplace.

Ode: The Music Makers
Arthur O'Shaughnessy

1. We are the music makers
And we are the dreamers of dreams,
Wandering by lone sea-breakers,
And sitting by desolate streams: -
World-losers and world-forsakers,
On whom the pale moon gleams:
Yet we are the movers and shakers
Of the world for ever, it seems.

2. With wonderful deathless ditties
We build up the world's great cities,
And out of a fabulous story
We fashion an empire's glory.
One man with a dream, at pleasure,
Shall go forth and conquer a crown;
And three with a new song's measure
Can trample a kingdom down.

3. We, in the ages lying
In the buried past of the earth,
Built Nineveh with our sighing,
And Babel itself in our mirth;
And o'erthrew them with prophesying
To the old of the new world's worth;
For each age is a dream that is dying,
Or one that is coming to birth.

4. A breath of our inspiration
Is the life of each generation:
A wondrous thing of our dreaming
Unearthly, impossible seeming -
The soldier, the king and the peasant
Are working together in one,
Till our dream shall become their present,
And their work in the world be done.

5. They had no vision amazing
Of the goodly house they are raising;
They had no divine foreshowing
Of the land to which they are going:
But on one man's soul it hath broken,
A light that doth not depart;
And his look, or a word he hath spoken,
Wrought flame in another man's heart.

6. And therefore to-day is thrilling
With a past day's late fulfilling;
And the multitudes are enlisted
In the faith that their fathers resisted
And, scorning the dream of tomorrow,
Are bringing to pass, as they may,
In the world, for its joy or its sorrow,
The dream that was scorned yesterday.

7. But we, with our dreaming and singing,
Ceaseless and sorrowless we!
The glory about us clinging
Of the glorious futures we see,
Our souls with high music ringing:
O men! it must ever be
That we dwell, in our dreaming and singing,
A little apart from ye.

8. For we are afar with the dawning
And the suns that are not yet high,
And out of the infinite morning
Intrepid you hear us cry -
How, spite of your human scorning,
Once more God's future draws nigh,
And already goes forth the warning
That ye of the past must die.

9. Great hail! we cry to the comers
From the dazzling unknown shore;
Bring us hither your sun and summers,
And renew our world as of yore;
You shall teach us your song's new numbers,
And things that we dreamed not before:
Yea, in spite of a dreamer who slumbers,
And a singer who sings no more.

ELGAR AND THE RELUCTANT ZOOLOGIST
SOME THOUGHTS ON *THE MUSIC MAKERS*

Edward Elgar's Op.69 *The Music Makers* is a setting for contralto, chorus and orchestra of an Ode by Arthur O'Shaughnessy. Dedicated "to my friend Nicholas Kilburn", it was completed on 21 August 1912 and premièred on 1 October 1912 with Muriel Foster as soloist and Elgar himself conducting at the Birmingham Festival.

Nicholas Kilburn (1843-1923) was by profession an iron merchant, but his first enthusiasm was for music. He was proficient on the organ, and also played piano and cello. He held a Mus.B. from Cambridge and a Mus.D. from Durham. He was founder and conductor of choral and orchestral societies in his home town of Bishop Auckland in County Durham, as well as Middlesbrough and Sunderland. A great admirer of Elgar, he organised numerous performances in the North East of England, conducting all the major works as they appeared. Elgar named him 'The Great Auk' (Bishop Auckland)! He was given to sending effusive letters to Elgar, and one supposes that the dedication was a supreme moment in his life.

Arthur O'Shaughnessy (1844-81) was born in London. A friend of Rosetti, he was employed on the staff of the British Museum (Department of Zoology) where - "near-sighted, uncoordinated and lacking in scientific fervour" according to a departmental report - he survived constant threats of dismissal. Superiors complained of his indiscipline and carelessness, and it was alleged he spent time drinking wine with students in his room! However, when subjected to an identification of lizards test in 1871, he passed with flying colours (only 3 wrong out of 60). He also published some perfectly sound scientific papers. He was never dismissed, but his promotion was blocked and the promise of a lectureship in the new South Kensington Building (The Natural History Museum) was never to materialise and, in any case, his death in January 1881 pre-dated the departmental move.

O'Shaughnessy was described by the young Edmund Gosse as "a sort of mystery, revealed twice a day. In the morning, a smart figure in a long frock coat with romantic eyes and bushy whiskers, he would be seen entering the monument and descending into its depths, to be observed no more till he swiftly rose and left it late in the afternoon." Clearly unfulfilled in his work, his main leisure activity was his writing. His ode *The Music Makers* appeared in *The Athenaeum* on 30 August 1873 and subsequently in his anthology *Music and Moonlight* (1874).

O'Shaughnessy's personal life was characterised, in the Victorian manner, by bereavement. His two sons died in infancy, and his wife within six years of the marriage. He himself soon followed in 1881 aged 36. Rather as Arthur Benson and *Land of Hope and Glory*, it is for *The Music Makers* verses, courtesy of Elgar, that he is now chiefly remembered.

Though it is interesting, in passing, to note that Elgar's has not been the only setting of O'Shaughnessy's verses. In 1964 the Hungarian composer Zoltan Kodaly, then aged 81, completed his setting of *The Music Makers* which was composed to mark the 700th anniversary of Merton College, Oxford. This little known work has now been recorded (see review in the *Elgar Society Journal*, July 2002). The Kodaly setting is on a much smaller scale than the Elgar. It has no soloist and lasts little more than ten minutes. Moreover it is quite different in mood. Both Robert Matthew-Walker's essay accompanying the CD and Paul Rooke's review in the *Elgar Society Journal* emphasise the contemplative, introspective, reminiscent nature of the Elgar in contrast to the vigorous, optimistic approach taken by Kodaly. I would add that it seems to me that Kodaly's is not only a far more straightforward setting of the text, but also, for those who know the Elgar, scarcely more than bland.

These verses - there are nine stanzas and Elgar set all of them without abridgement or alteration, the first time he had followed such a practice in a major work since 1889 - are often regarded as weak, though Michael Kennedy has argued they are no worse than plenty of others set by great composers. Clearly they appealed to Elgar, who was more interested in musical suitability and, especially, finding words to serve his very personal purposes, than in poetic quality. As Dr Patrick Little has observed in his essay *Songs of Love and Death* (*Elgar Society Journal*, March 1996), "I suspect that for Elgar, as long as certain minimal standards were maintained, his real interest was in finding words which said what he wanted to say".

A characteristic not frequently discussed is that they are both ambiguous and, at times, patent nonsense. The notion of the world's musicians "with wonderful deathless ditties", building "the world's great cities" and fashioning "an empire's story" would, one feels, cut little ice with the great Machiavellian Statesmen of History - the Bismarcks, the Bonapartes.

At least readers would agree that O'Shaughnessy's verses are in praise of music and the makers of music - indeed, as I have just contended, it seems to me at times a patent overstatement of the musician's role. It is affirmative and optimistic writing. But that is not what we get from Elgar - *The Music Makers* is not his *Ode to Joy*. Consider the very opening, the Prelude: " ... almost an

Left:
A copy of the original
Novello vocal score of
The Music Makers,
autographed by Elgar.

Below:
Nicholas Kilburn

anthology of his (Elgar's) characteristics" writes Diana McVeagh, while Michael Kennedy has argued that it contains "the melody that is perhaps the most Elgarian expression of yearning in all his music." And containing already the quotation of the 'Enigma' Variations theme, used "because it expressed when written (in 1898) my sense of the loneliness of the artist as described in the first six lines of the ode, and, to me, it still embodies that sense. At the end of my full score of the Variations I wrote 'Bramo assai, poco spero, nulla cheggio' (Tasso) - 'I long for much, I hope for little, I ask for nothing'. This was true in 1898 and might be written with equal truth at the end of this work in 1912", wrote Elgar to Ernest Newman. At the end of the prelude the chorus enters pianissimo - "probably the simplest choral music he ever composed", observes Diana McVeagh. The scene is set for much of what is to follow.

Certainly Elgar laboured over the composition of *The Music Makers*, having been working at such a project intermittently since 1903. Jaeger refers to the project in a letter of 1904 as *The Dreamers*, and permission to set the O'Shaughnessy Ode was, in fact, obtained in 1908. Given Elgar's use of quotations from his own works in *The Music Makers*, it would, of course, have been a rather different work had he finished it promptly since works such as the Violin Concerto and Second Symphony were not extant! But then, perhaps, we should have had a different 'Enigma' Variations line-up had that work been composed twenty years later.

As the work neared completion in 1912 Alice Elgar dutifully records Edward's struggles: "May 30th 1912. E. going on with his work - Not very happy over it - Gives A. a pain in her heart for him to be so tensed". And at the moment of the completion of the vocal score (19 July), Edward wrote famously to Alice Stuart Wortley: "I sent the last page to the printers. Alice and Carice were away for the day and I wandered alone on the heath - it was bitterly cold - I wrapped myself in a thick overcoat & sat for two minutes, tears streaming out of my cold eyes and loathed the world, came back to the house - empty and cold - how I hated having written anything: so I wandered out again & shivered & longed to destroy the work of my hands - all wasted. And this was to have been the one real day in my artistic life - sympathy at the end of work. 'World losers & world forsakers for ever & ever'. How true it is."

The première was shared with the first English performance of Sibelius's Fourth Symphony conducted by the composer - great days in Birmingham to have such giants there. Alice, as usual, was in a transport of delight: "Most splendid and impressive. Wonderful effects of Orchestration & Chorus beautiful rendering. Muriel splendid. E. conducted magnificently. Had a great reception". But the critics were less sure and O'Shaughnessy's poem was considered by a number to be irrelevant to the twentieth century.

However, Robin Legge of the *Daily Telegraph* was very perceptive. He heard in the work a mood of "unsatisfied yearning" and observed "the composer seems to long himself to be convinced that the music makers are what the poet represents them to be; if they are, then surely here is a case of the most glorious optimism ... where the poet speaks in general terms, Elgar appears to look at the personal aspect of the matter". Legge certainly did not find the "optimism" of the Ode much represented in the music, and I think he very much put his finger on the core of the matter.

Opinion about the work, even among eminent Elgarians, has remained divided ever since. Diana McVeagh found it a "pleasant work to sing but not quite so satisfying to listen to". Despite certain virtues it is "pretentious" and "only in a superficial sense catches the spirit of the poem". It was repetitive and its themes often "undistinguished". Diana's influential study of Elgar (*Edward Elgar: His Life and Music*), incredible though it seems, was written more than 45 years ago. Today, in fact, she tells me that she finds it "a very moving work" which "tells us more about EE than about O'S", whereas in 1955 she regarded it simply as "a good setting of the poem, not a re-creation". Certainly I agree with Diana's current position and not the original one. Indeed it seems to me that Elgar's is not a good "setting" of the poem, but whether good, bad or indifferent it is certainly a "re-creation". Elgar himself in a letter to Ernest Newman (dated 14 August 1912) observed: "occasionally I have departed from general interpretation of the words, as an orator leaves the broad view of his subject to give a particular instance". Yes, indeed, and one could say that was an understatement!

A more enthusiastic commentator has been Michael Kennedy. He finds Elgar's use of self-quotation "deeply moving" and in "perfect taste". The whole is original and "one of Elgar's most endearing and unjustly underrated works".

More than seven years before the première of *The Music Makers*, Elgar had already made a stab at articulating his musical/artistic credo, and coincidentally also in Birmingham. On 16 March 1905 he had delivered his inaugural lecture as Peyton Professor of Music at the city's university, and entitled it 'A Future For English Music'. Elgar's tenure of the chair was brief - just over 3 years - and his role was pretty much limited to the delivery of some eight public lectures between March 1905 and November 1906. It is generally thought that he was like a fish out of water in this role, though there is no doubt he made considerable efforts to fulfil what was an uncongenial task. In the Inaugural Lecture he quickly struck an enlightened/progressive note: " ... the art that stands still is dead: the art that moves, or I would rather say progresses, is alive". But he had, of course, posed the question of what is progress and what mere movement? He certainly argued that there was evidence of healthy movement in England, though he conspicuously did not specify names of young progressives. Rather he paid a fulsome tribute to Parry and made a sly dig - at least it was widely taken as such - at Stanford. Certainly, too, there were plenty of things of which the young needed to beware or avoid:

1. Self-proclaimed modernists - those who say " 'we are modern and we are in the race': when as a matter of fact they are quite out of the running ... singing revolutionary songs to the wrong tune".
2. The desire among the young for "notoriety". There was no need in England in 1905 for eccentric excesses such as in France where the writer Gautier sported a red waistcoat.
3. Disrespect for "older institutions to which in the past we owe so much and in the future we look for further help and enlightenment".
4. Imitations - eg of Richard Strauss by those "careful to avoid all that is melodious and I will add sublime", and also of the "anaemic followers of the modern French School".

It hardly sounds very revolutionary! Elgar went on to urge the young to be "true to themselves, cease from imitation and draw inspiration from their own land"; this is a strange injunction from one who, though certainly true to himself, drew influences from Germany especially, and from Purcell and English folk music virtually not at all. Did he mean the Malvern Hills? At all events he threw in his own credo about music being "broad, chivalrous, noble, healthy and above all an out-of-door sort of spirit". One can see the applicability of this to his own music, but perhaps words like "chivalrous" and "out-of-door" were not of much general help!

In a peroration Elgar opined that "We (ie musicians) speak a loftier language than mere human speech, in the wondrous accents of Music ... We place our lever in heaven and by it we can move the world". Shades of O'Shaughnessy here:

> Yet we are the movers and shakers
> Of the world for ever, it seems".

The reaction to the lecture was mixed, and certainly included disapproval and puzzlement. Clearly it was something of a rag-bag, and included something for everybody.

There is, however, another - and more immediate - literary source specifically concerning Elgar's reaction to *The Music Makers* text. Ernest Newman was to write the programme analysis for the Birmingham première and he requested Elgar's aid. This led to the letter dated 14 August 1912 and an enclosed "introductory note" from Elgar. I have already referred to it twice - for Elgar's explanation of his use of the 'Enigma' theme, and secondly his admission that periodically he had departed from the general nature of O'Shaughnessy's words to make personal points. It should be pointed out, of course, that one needs to be careful when dealing with the writings and speeches of Edward Elgar. So long as it is borne in mind that we are dealing with a notoriously thin-skinned person of volatile swings in mood, who frequently exaggerated, said things which were patent nonsense and/or he later regretted, that he was not averse to being economical with the truth, and the while deliberately sprayed red herrings right and left - then no doubt Elgar's writings are wonderful primary sources. It seems to me that his programme notes for the Second Symphony (letter to Littleton of Novello 13 April 1911) are almost calculated to mislead. An entire study could be made of this and myriad other examples! Elgar never wrote an autobiography. Had he done so it would have been, I suspect, as useless to the historian as the majority of the genre. One might be tempted to add that even the memoirs of some of those who knew him have done as much to impede as to assist our knowledge, and thus understanding, of Edward.

Still let us consider the Newman letter and programme notes a little further. It is interesting that Elgar claims to invest the interpolation of the *Marseillaise* and *Rule Britannia* with "deadly sarcasm" on the words "empire's glory". Indeed he cannot resist going on to observe that under the current Liberal government *Rule Britannia* "has been made the most foolish of all national boasts". It is interesting, too, that he spells out the significance of the 'Nimrod' quotation, a tribute to Jaeger's memory: " ... amongst all the inept writing and wrangling about music his voice was clear, ennobling, sober and sane". Elgar writes, too, of the mission of the artist/composer "to renew the world as of yore" (to quote O'Shaughnessy), but what is important is that for Edward the musical consequence of this is that "the atmosphere of the music" should for the most part be "sad", and that even the moments of enthusiasm and bursts of joy are to be equated with "moods which the creative artist suffers in creating ... yes, suffers, this is the only word I dare use".

None the less, Elgar's final paragraph seems firmly back in line with O'Shaughnessy: "The mainspring of O'Shaughnessy's Ode is the sense of progress, of never ceasing change; it is the duty of the artist to see that this inevitable change is progress. With a deep sense of this trust, I have endeavoured to interpret the Ode as shewing the continuity of art, in spite of those dreamers and singers who dream and sing 'no more'". Though even here Elgar hints at what was to be a major pre-occupation for him, ie dreaming and singing <u>no more</u>.

I gave my view earlier that O'Shaughnessy's poem is to an extent ambiguous, and herein lay Elgar's opportunity. Though there are elements of nostalgia, it is essentially a work of "impulsive, heroic optimism". But there is no doubt that what Elgar did was to sieze upon certain lines as the fount of his inspiration:

> And sitting by desolate streams;
> World-losers and world forsakers
>
> And a singer who sings no more
>
> The dream that was scorned yesterday
>
> That we dwell in our dreaming and singing
> A little apart from ye
>
> And their work in the world is done
> That ye of the past must die

It is with such passages that the mood of the composition lies. Robert Anderson has argued that Elgar was "hardly faithful to the poem's intent", and in emphasising the past composes "a personal document of almost painful intensity".

Then, too, there is the notion of "dreams" and "dreaming", a recurrent leitmotif in Elgar's music. There are ten usages of *dream/dreaming/dreamer* in the poem - a considerable attraction for Elgar one might think! But what does the notion of *dreaming* convey - an ideal not yet attained but towards which we aspire, or a lost and vanished world, gone past and not to be recaptured or recreated? Let it be noticed here that only twelve months earlier the Rondo of the Second Symphony had been a "nightmare" rather than "dream", and in *The Music Makers* when Elgar thinks of dreams it is *The Dream of Gerontius* and of Gerontius's moment of death.

I have mentioned Elgar's interpolation of the 'Nimrod' Variation tune as a tribute to Jaeger. This stands at (and as?) the core of the work, following hard upon the soloist's entry (Novello Edition Vocal Score, p.41 F49) and set to the words:

> But on one man's soul it hath broken,
> A light that doth not depart;

It is a glorious moment, especially when the tune is coupled with the coda of the Second Symphony.

But what are we to make of it? How affirmative is it? Elgar specifically assures Newman (the famous letter again) that: "I do not mean to convey that his was the only soul on which light had broken or that his was the only word, or look that wrought 'flame in another man's heart'". However, the fact remains that he did choose at this point to highlight the stature of one individual, and he fairly recently dead (1909). It may also be purely coincidential that 90 years and two World Wars on it is scarcely possible for anyone in the English-speaking Commonwealth to hear that tune without calling to mind all sorts of associations of elegy, loss and mourning. It would be interesting to know to what extent 'Nimrod' had between 1899 and 1912 acquired the extra-musical associations from which it is now inseparable. Did Elgar in 1912 know the effect it was destined to have?

Let us consider Elgar's setting of the seventh stanza (Vocal Score p.60 F70).

> But we, with our dreaming and singing,
> Ceaseless and sorrowless we!
> The glory about us clinging
> Of the glorious futures we see,
> Our souls with high music ringing:

What could be more affirmative? But then O'Shaughnessy gives Elgar his chance as he continues:

> O men! it must ever be
> That we dwell, in our dreaming and singing,
> A little apart from ye.

So it is that we get, it seems to me, much about the loneliness of the composer and not so much "high music" and "glorious future", nor a setting of "sorrowless" which conveys lack of sorrow - quite the reverse!

Listeners, one hopes, will notice in this passage the 'Enigma' quote yet again, and also quotations from the Violin Concerto of 1910 at the words "in our dreaming and singing, a little apart". What are we to associate with this? Windflowers and Souls enshrined within? Alice Stuart Wortley? Is Elgar seeking solace in the remembrance of friends, as Simon Mundy has suggested? Do we pick up Robert Anderson's reminder that the nobilmente passage from the slow movement here quoted is what Edward told Ivor Atkins he wished to have engraved on his tombstone? Do we simply think of one of the most wistful things in all Elgar?

In fact, of course, many listeners at performances of *The Music Makers* will not make any such connections. They will never even have heard Elgar's Violin Concerto and, doubtless, this applies to the chorus as well. It is, of course, the use of self-quotation from his works which more obviously than anything else makes this so personal a statement from Elgar. He himself (the Newman letter again) assures us that: "If these quoted passages are unknown, the music may be listened to simply as an expression of feelings called up by the poem, without regard to the quotations as such". Clearly for listeners in this position this is all that <u>can</u> be done; but at what loss! Michael Kennedy has pointed out that the quotations represent only a small part of the whole, and frequently we are reminded that self-quotation is a common currency among composers of the Romantic period, reference usually being made to Richard Strauss and especially *Ein Heldenleben*, and to Mahler. But this does not mean there is no problem with *The Music Makers*, and it is clear, as Diana McVeagh has observed, that biographical knowledge of Elgar and acquaintance with a fair amount of his music is vitally important for the listener.

No doubt some of the quotations are not so very important. The fleeting reference to *Rule Britannia* never actually seems audible in performances, nor do I think the reminder from *Sea Pictures* at the words "sea breakers" in the first stanza is crucial. It is, of course, always nice from the standpoint of one-up-manship to recognise these things - those (few?) people in the audience who recognise Britten's quotation from *Tristan* at an appropriately comic moment in *Albert Herring* invariably laugh very loudly. But with *The Music Makers* there is more to it, and I suggest that if you find yourself at a performance without knowing something of *Gerontius*, 'Enigma' Variations, the Violin Concerto, the First Symphony etc., then you <u>do</u> have a problem, and it cannot be blinked.

Michael Kennedy in a useful appendix to *Portrait of Elgar* certainly is helpful when he lists exactly at which point the quotations occur. But Michael, too, has written elsewhere (programme notes in Adrian Boult BBC Promenade 90th Birthday tribute): "As one comes to know the work more intimately, one keeps on noticing what seem to be other quotations - are they intentional or are they merely Elgarian turns of phrase, tantalisingly familiar?" This seems fair comment and none of us can be complacent when it comes to thinking we have finally got the measure of it all!

Doubtless it is this problem of the use of so many quotations which has contributed to *The Music Makers'* somewhat equivocal position regarding popularity. Even today one cannot think of it as one of the great front-line popular favourites. It seems to me that when Linda Maria Koldau in the *Elgar Society Journal* argues that, perhaps, the work is too personal to be understood by anybody else but Elgar and his closest friends, she has a point!

Certainly if you are thinking of introducing someone to Edward's music, my advice is not to begin here! *The Music Makers* is a work which Elgarians should come to late, after lengthy familiarisation with Edward's life and works.

Be that as it may, I dare say that the quotation from the First Symphony, when we hear that work's great motto theme, is fairly well-known. We are in the eighth stanza (Vocal Score p.68 F.78):

> For we are afar with the dawning
> And the suns that are not yet high,

Not for the first or last time Elgar employs the tune of the opening chorus; what has come to represent "a sort of artist's theme" (Newman letter). Then we have the words:

> And out of the infinite morning
> Intrepid you hear us cry -
> How, spite of your human scorning,
> Once more God's future draws nigh.

It is here we get the remembrance of the First Symphony, very much fortissimo. Could words be more affirmative and inspiring - "infinite" and "morning", "intrepid" and "God's future"? And Edward does O'Shaughnessy proud. It is an overwhelming moment. Quite apart from the sound, when we think of the First Symphony we surely recall Elgar's letter to Walford Davies (13 November 1908): "There is no programme beyond a wide experience of human life with a great charity (love) & a <u>massive</u> hope in the future". And here I do think Edward is accurate about his own music!

However, the mood is not long sustained. Jerrold Northrop Moore writes that the big tune only "flashed as spasmodic inspiration and was gone". What we have, argues Linda Maria Koldau, is the sense of "flashing inspiration vanishing immediately". To be followed by:

> And already goes forth the warning
> That ye of the past must die.

Surely we have a strong sense that Elgar, who spent much of his life complaining/believing that no one wanted <u>his</u> music any more, finds these the key lines which cannot be resisted. Clearly the poet means that the past is to be overtaken by a glorious future, ever onwards and upwards, but it sounds very much as if Elgar is pre-occupied with death rather than re-birth. Consider the setting of the word "die" and the orchestral passage which follows.

I have already alluded to the mood in which Elgar found himself at the completion of the composition of *The Music Makers* - his letter of 12 August 1912 to Alice Stuart Wortley, bemoaning life outdoors on Hampstead Heath and the inhospitably cold house to which he returned. The Elgars had moved into Severn House, Hampstead, on New Year's Day 1912 and Edward was soon regretting parting from Herefordshire and Worcestershire. By 1912 he was at the height of his musical powers and had 'enjoyed', after years of anonymity, a public recognition and adulation quite unprecedented. Assuredly, however, it had not brought peace of mind, nor, I suspect, did he feel it had brought commensurate financial reward. By the autumn of that year it was being borne in on him that the move to Hampstead may have been the inevitable consequence of his fame and national status, but that it was a price to be paid, not a harbinger of content.

Michael Kennedy has argued Elgar's "homesickness" at this time, and also tosses in for good measure the loss of the *Titanic* as a further cause for depression. Edward's depressions were, of course, frequent and he tended to bounce back remarkably. But such moods were surely increasing. There must be dozens of examples. In 1904 he wrote to Schuster: "I am still very low and see nothing in the future but a black, stone wall"; in 1905 to Jaeger: "I have no news of myself as I have for ever lost interest in that person"; in 1907 to Walford Davies: "Now I see nothing ahead". Elgar in 1912 was 55 years old, and had seen younger friends such as Rodewald (1903) and Jaeger (1909) die. The very day on which he had finished the full score Canon Gorton, another long-standing friend, plunged in his invalid chair into the Wye in flood in Hereford. The body was not found for ten days. Early in 1913, though there is evidence that her friends knew or suspected this somewhat earlier, Julia Worthington was diagnosed as suffering from cancer. It rapidly proved terminal. Michael Kennedy observes in *Portrait of Elgar* that Edward was by now a "deeply divided, unhappy man. He had lost his faith in God and now he had no faith in man's redemption". Little wonder that he was not the ideal person in 1912 to draw inspiration from the words: "Once more God's future draws nigh"!

It is notable that the two great works which preceded *The Music Makers* - the Violin Concerto (1910) and the Second Symphony (1911) - are also characterised by a mood of autumnal longing and sad retrospection. In one of his most famous observations about *The Music Makers* Edward linked it to these other two works: "I have written out my soul in the Concerto, Symphony II and the Ode ... in these 3 works I have shewn myself" (letter to Alice Stuart Wortley 29 August 1912). It is, however, amusing to note in passing a letter of Elgar's to the dedicatee, Kilburn, a few months later (26

March 1913). Kilburn had put on a performance with his Bishop Auckland Music Society and wrote to Edward in his usual enthusiastic tone. Edward was - one is tempted to say 'as usual' - unwell and delayed his reply for ten days: " ... so ill have I been & so sick am I still". He observed that Kilburn's letter had talked "mysteriously as becomes you & your northern atmosphere", claimed that he could not follow it and observed that "the whole thing (no matter how one fights and avoids it) is merely commercial". What did he mean? If that the writing of *The Music Makers* was inspired by no more than a commercial motive, then one is amazed as no doubt Kilburn was by this reply. In fact it is another classic example of when not to believe Elgar! The safest thing is to listen to the music.

Not only has *The Music Makers* never achieved wide popularity but also it has never been much written about. In twenty years there was never anything said about it, other than in passing, at the London Branch of the Elgar Society until Richard Westwood-Brookes spoke about Kilburn in 1997. Obviously the standard works - Northrop Moore, Kennedy, McVeagh, Anderson, etc. - discuss the work, but it is virtually ignored so far as articles in learned musical magazines go. Geoffrey Hodgkins has brought out a remarkable *Elgar Bibliography* listing all such things to the end of 1992 and this reveals just one article entitled *Arthur O'Shaughnessy and The Music Makers* by Stanley Holmes in what was then the *Elgar Society Newsletter* in 1975. This, in fact, amounts to a useful, albeit brief, biographical note on O'Shaughnessy.

However, there is one other article, already mentioned, by Linda Maria Koldau in the *Elgar Society Journal* for January 1993. She was at the time spending a year with Dr Christopher Kent at Reading University and, we are told, "not yet 21" and an undergraduate in Germany. The article has been rightly praised. It is perceptive and well-argued. I have already called her in support of the view of the intensely personal nature of the work; her view that, perhaps, only Elgar and his intimates could really understand it. It is not a work, she goes on to argue, which lends itself to the norm of aesthetic criticism. Elgar forces our attention on himself rather than on the music: "when the artist's personality becomes more important than his work, the crucial point of music as a medium that can speak for itself is lost". Her conclusion is that it is at this point that she longs to go back to those times when the composer was of smallest importance to the aesthetic understanding of his work. "A true work of art," she concludes, "must have a life of its own, disentangled from its creator's personality".

Now with this I do not agree. Far be it for me to challenge the classical school of compositon; I was an ardent Mozartian years before I heard either of Elgar's Symphonies or Concertos, and devoted I remain. But to uphold the one does not mean one need reject the other. I think Fraulein Koldau's philosophy might lead us to reject vast chunks of romantic music - not just Elgar, but also Strauss and Mahler again come rapidly to mind and there are many more. Certainly it is a view which Elgar is on record as not sharing. To quote the letter to Newman once again, and for the last time: "I am glad you like the idea of the quotations: after all art must be the man, & all true art is, to a great extent, egotism".

Linda Maria Koldau, however, certainly declares her position, and it is time for me to sum up mine. Essentially I have laboured two points.

Firstly that throughout *The Music Makers*, even if apparently at odds with O'Shaughnessy's words, there runs a vein of sadness, regret, wistfulness, longing, yearning. Now this is, to put it mildly, all right by me! Elgar was a wide-ranging composer and, indeed, I react with pleasure to the music of pomp and circumstance, patriotism and Empire; similarly to his wonderful empathy with the young and thus to works like *The Wand of Youth* Suites, the *Nursery Suite*, the splendid *Starlight Express* music. Who would be without the great Oratorios or the tone poems, *Cockaigne* with all its wit and ebullience, *In the South* with its evocation of Italy? But ultimately it is this vein of sadness/regret that above all inhabits the greatest works of his great period. I have observed that *The Music Makers* was preceded by the Violin Concerto and the Second Symphony, works of similar mood; it was, of course, followed by the Symphonic Study *Falstaff* and the Cello Concerto which continue the line, and on to the late Chamber works.

Diana McVeagh puts it better than I can: "Right through his music (certainly of his greatest period) runs a philosophy, touched at times with wistfulness, at times a fervent threnody, yet always humane and with ultimate consolation, that is fundamental and enduring ... In him the bloom of full summer has ripened into the rich yet regretful fall of the autumn".

And though *The Music Makers* might be a very personal work, Elgar in this mood does strike resonances with so many because his sense of passing time, of a vanishing past, of life's regrets and missed turnings is a common currency. What a great genius can, of course, do is to articulate thoughts to which we respond, but which we ourselves cannot express so memorably or movingly.

Because Elgar in this vein speaks so clearly to me, I am glad that *The Music Makers* is what I take it to be - another in this Elgarian canon, and not some trivial setting of vacuous and naively optimistic words. I suggested, in passing, at the outset that *The Music Makers* was not Elgar's 'Ode to Joy'. Could anyone since Beethoven's 'Choral' Symphony (and then it needed a

Beethoven) sensibly seek to aspire to any such thing given the collapse of 18th Century Enlightenment in the disillusion which followed the French Revolution, and all that has ensued right into and through the 20th Century? A work like Ireland's setting on the very eve of World War II of *These Things Shall Be*, with its talk of "loftier races than e'er the world has known" and "loftier music" filling the skies, has always seemed to me absurd. Fortunately Elgar, perhaps in spite of "good intentions", was incapable in 1912 of penning platitudes. His music, certainly his major undertakings, by this time, as William Mann has observed of the Second Symphony, was about "a fine man, deeply disturbed by the times he lived in, terrified by the future".

Secondly I have emphasised the personal nature of the work, with its myriad self-quotation. It is this which Linda Maria Koldau in the end could not accept, observing "I am probably one of the 'unsympathetic' mentioned by Kennedy". Well, yes, I think she is! I hope that by now she will have heard a lot more Elgar and read a lot more about him, and then she might find her reservations unimportant. I have no such reservations. I was not born when Elgar died, but I have heard him speak and seen him move (on film), seen hundreds of photographs and a number of portraits. I have recordings of him conducting his own music. I have read numerous books and articles about him. I have read lots of his letters (and, indeed, possess a few). I have wrestled to try to read his often barely legible handwriting, and that of his wife. (Carice is better!). I have heard all the distinguished Elgar scholars of the day speak about him. I have been in the house in which he was born, and also the ones in which he composed the Violin Concerto and the Chamber Music; the Hampstead mansion, like the house in Worcester in which he died, has been demolished! I have walked the Malverns and been to so many places associated with him. If Linda Maria Koldau feels that *The Music Makers* can only speak to Elgar himself or his friends, well I am making a claim to membership of the latter category. For those who love Elgar's music and also Edward himself - and despite all his foibles, perhaps because of them, he was an endlessly fascinating and lovable man - that *The Music Makers* tells us less about O'Shaughnessy's aspirations than about Elgar is no problem at all. For Elgarians *The Music Makers* is surely a crucial and unique work.

In conclusion consider the setting of the final stanza. The soloist begins with a bold declaration of the lines:

> Great hail! we cry to the comers
> From the dazzling unknown shore;

and the wonderful second tune of the prelude, that which Michael Kennedy called "the melody that is perhaps the most Elgarian expression of yearning in all his music", is brought in to accompany the words:

> Bring us hither your sun and your summers
> And renew our world as of yore

Gradually there seems to be a growing optimism as we move to:

> You shall teach us your song's new numbers,
> And things that we dreamed not before:

But imperceptibly, four bars before F.92, we find the Chorus is back in the seventh stanza, and though the soloist reminds us of "high music ringing", it is now that the Chorus enters with a reprise of the words:

> O men! it must ever be
> That we dwell, in our dreaming and singing,
> A little apart from ye.

By F.95 we are back with "You shall teach us", etc. and the mood becomes affirmative again. At F.97 we even get a recurrence of the Chorus's inspirational:

> For we are afar with the dawning
> And the suns that are not yet high

from stanza 8. It does not, however, go on to a reprise of the big triumphant tune of the First Symphony.

The work is not destined to end on any note of false optimism. In fact it is heartbreaking! The soloist tells us of "the singer who sings no more", and we have Elgar's last quotation "Novissima hora est" - the very death cry of Gerontius - in the orchestra. Perhaps, suggests Diana McVeagh, an allusion to "Elgar's awareness of his own mortality, or more widely of the short human span of all artists". The Chorus dejectedly mutter "no more", and the end comes with a final reprise of the opening chorus "We are the Music Makers", the theme drained of all feeling of affirmation. It is, as Michael Kennedy writes, "the music of a man of sorrows, acquainted with grief".

BIBLIOGRAPHY

Anderson, Robert : *Elgar* (J.M.Dent, London, 1993)

Holmes, S.C.A. : *Arthur O'Shaughnessy and 'The Music Makers'* (*Elgar Society Newsletter*, 1975)

Kennedy, Michael : *Portrait of Elgar* (2nd Edition Oxford University Press, 1982)

Koldau, Linda Maria : *Elgar's 'The Music Makers : The Problem of Aesthetic Assessment* (*Elgar Society Journal*, January 1993)

McVeagh, Diana : *Edward Elgar : His Life and Music* (J.M.Dent, London 1955)

Moore, Jerrold Northrop : *Edward Elgar : A Creative Life* (Oxford University Press, 1984)

Moore, Jerrold Northrop : *Elgar and His Publishers : Letters of a Creative Life* (Oxford University Press, 1987)

Moore, Jerrold Northrop : *Edward Elgar : Letters of a Lifetime* (Oxford University Press, 1990)

Mundy, Simon : *Elgar : His Life and Times* (Midas Books, Tunbridge Wells, 1980)

Young, Percy M. : *Elgar O.M.* (White Lion Publishers, London 1973)

Young, Percy M. : *A Future For English Music : and Other Lectures by Edward Elgar* (Dennis Dobson, London, 1968)

NOTE

I have also made reference to Concert Programme Notes written by Michael Kennedy, Diana McVeagh and William Mann. I am grateful, too, to Diana McVeagh for sharing her views on *The Music Makers* in a personal letter to me.

Anyone interested in studying *The Music Makers* is advised to refer to the score (published by Novello & Co., London), and to recordings. The recording conducted by Sir Adrian Boult (London Philharmonic Orchestra and Chorus with Janet Baker as soloist) issued by EMI in 1967 (EMI CDS 7 47208 8) and that conducted by Andrew Davis in August 1993 with the BBC Symphony Orchestra and Chorus with Jean Rigby as soloist (Teldec 4509-92374-2), can be warmly recommended.

The recording of Kodaly's *The Music Makers*, with the Orchestra and Choir of the Oxford Orchestra da Camera, conductor Howard Williams, is issued by Somm (SOMMCD 230). The CD also includes a perfectly good version of the Elgar setting, with Christina Wilson as soloist.

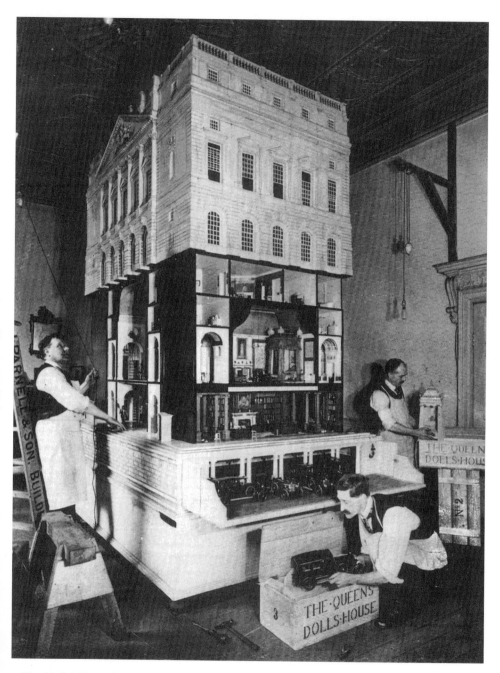

The Dolls' House being prepared for transportation to the Empire Exhibition at Wembley

ELGAR AND QUEEN MARY'S DOLLS' HOUSE

As the Great War drew to a close, Elgar was sunk in depression. On 5 November 1918 he replied to a request from Binyon that he set an Ode about peace: "I do not feel drawn to write peace music somehow ... if anything could draw me your poem would, but the whole atmosphere is too full of complexities for me to feel music to it: not the atmosphere of the poem but of the time I mean". In April 1920 there came Alice's death - the slow movement of the Quartet her graveside requiem. Elgar's career had begun what Michael Kennedy called its "long and slow diminuendo"; likening Elgar's existence to a passage in *Antony and Cleopatra* - "The music, ho! ... Let it alone; let's to billiards". Literally to billiards at Severn House - except that Severn House itself was up for sale and by September 1921 he was preparing to leave. Earlier, in August, he had left Brinkwells for the last time, while Carice's engagement in March of the same year presaged increased loneliness. She married Samuel Blake in January 1922.

On 22 October 1921 Elgar wrote a remarkable and petulant letter to Troyte Griffith; Troyte, of course, was an architect and Elgar's letter was concerned in part with the greatest architect of the day, Sir Edwin Landseer Lutyens.

I can't make Lutyens out: he seems to advertise more than ever. I had a circular asking me to contribute a microscopic MS to help furnish a Doll's House Castle, or something, wh: he designs to present to the Queen - Everybody is being asked to contribute a work of art (miniature) or piece of furniture for this senseless scheme - I refused tout court -

That Elgar was greatly affronted at the Dolls' House approach is confirmed by the fact that he was still losing no opportunity - indeed availing himself of totally inappropriate opportunity - to complain several months later. Siegfried Sassoon recalls in his diary (8 June 1922) making up a party at Schuster's Thameside retreat, the Hut at Bray, in early June 1922 - in fact Sunday 4th. Elgar was present and "delivered himself of a petulant tirade which culminated in a crescendo climax of rudeness aimed at Lady Maud" (ie Lady Maud Warrender): "'I started with nothing, and I have made a position for myself! We all know that the King and Queen are incapable of appreciating anything artistic; they've never asked for the full score of my Second Symphony to be added to the library at Windsor. But as the crown of my career I'm asked to contribute to a DOLLS' HOUSE for the QUEEN! I've been a monkey-on-a-stick for you people long enough. Now I'm getting off the stick. I wrote and said that I hoped they wouldn't have the impertinence to press the matter any further. I consider it an insult for an artist to be asked to mix himself up in such nonsense'."

Elgar was backed up by Robert Nicholls (1893-1944), a minor poet on leave from his appointment as Professor of English Literature in the Imperial University, Tokyo, who had not been invited to contribute to the Dolls' House, and now chimed in with observations about "the seriousness of his art" and "the rottenness of an Age which concentrates its efforts on Dolls' Houses". But one guesses that most of the company were as astonished as Sassoon at Elgar's outburst.

Sassoon's account can clearly be only a paraphrase of what Elgar said but, recalled within a couple of days of the incident, it can be taken as pretty accurate. Sassoon, though finding Elgar the man extremely irritating in this post-war manifestation, was a devotee of his music - especially *The Apostles* and the Violin Concerto, which latter he records by July 1923 he had heard eleven times. Conventional wisdom, too, might lead one to think Sassoon at that time less of an 'establishment figure' than Elgar, having published, while still a serving Officer, a famous protest against the War in July 1917, and followed this by throwing the ribbon of his Military Cross into the Mersey. Notwithstanding, he proved perfectly willing when approached to contribute an item to the Dolls' House.

One is left, too, to wonder at the reaction of the unfortunate Lady Maud Warrender. This handsome, aristocratic and musically talented lady - she had sung the solo part in *The Music Makers* - was a close friend of Queen Alexandra, the Queen Mother, as well as an intimate of Queen Mary; her brother was Comptroller of the Queen's Household (1901-22) and subsequently her son was appointed Vice-Chamberlain to George V. She herself was much involved in the Dolls' House project. By now she was a long-standing friend and benefactor of Elgar. She had been along with Elgar in the party which in 1905 was entertained by Lord Charles Beresford to a Mediterranean Cruise, was the dedicatee of Elgar's song *Pleading* composed in 1908, and Elgar was a frequent guest at her home near Rye. Perhaps surprisingly, the friendship was not permanently prejudiced by Elgar's outburst and, ironically, she was subsequently to be found interceding with the King and Queen to afford patronage at a concert in 1933 at the Wigmore Hall to mark the composer's 76th birthday.

The idea of the Queen Mary's Dolls' House was conceived in the spring of 1921 by Princess Marie Louise (b.1872), granddaughter of Victoria and first cousin to George V, a woman of considerable artistic interests and connections. The Queen had a veritable mania for collecting miniature objects ("tiny craft") and, indeed, was notorious for her open admiration of the possessions of other people who, thus, felt constrained to offer the coveted object as a gift to the delighted collector. One was well-advised to conceal valuables if the Queen was paying a visit - a stratagem widely practiced in Society circles. A magnificent Dolls' House, therefore, seemed an ideal gift to express the gratitude of the Nation at the role of the King and Queen during the war years. At the same time, it was soon realised, such a project would fit in admirably as an advertisement for Britain and British achievements at the planned British Empire Exhibition which was to take place at Wembley in the spring of 1924 and which was to proclaim Britain's re-emergence in the post-war world.

Among Princess Marie Louise's artistic friends was the great architect Sir Edwin Landseer Lutyens whose commissions encompassed projects ranging from Hampstead Garden Suburb to the Government Buildings at New Delhi. She waylaid him at the private viewing of the Royal Academy's Summer Exhibition of 1921: "Sned, I want you to do me a favour. Will you design me a dolls' house for Queen Mary?" Lutyens ('Ned' to his intimates!) agreed and soon developed a positive enthusiasm for the project, which he conceived as enabling "future generations to see how a King and Queen of England lived in the 20th Century and what authors, artists and craftsmen there were of note during their reign". He embarked eagerly on the three-year project. The

Edwin Lutyens, R.A.

Dolls' House was to be on a scale of 1":12", and to be a fantastically detailed and accurate working model. There were to be lifts, hot and cold running water, water closets, electric lights, clocks, etc., etc., all in working order. Virtually every item of furnishing was specially commissioned, and the notion was that the undertaking be financed by gift and donations. Lutyens, notwithstanding, made a considerable personal financial commitment, guaranteeing £11,000 and actually spending, unknown to his wife, £6,300 which he did not recover until the House was successfully exhibited - this at the time when Elgar's real house/mansion in Hampstead was on the market for £7,000 and failing to find a buyer! Queen Mary, meanwhile, once appraised of the suggestion, shared the architect's enthusiasm and made regular visits to Lutyen's house in Mansfield Street where the entire drawing room had been given over to the project.

Of special interest was the library which measured 45" long, 21" wide and 15.5" high. Panelled in Italian walnut, it contained 350 leather-bound and specially written volumes, embossed with the letter 'M'. The Princess wrote personally to 171 authors soliciting contributions in their own hand. Conan-Doyle contributed an original story of 500 words, while Kipling's item - several of his poems illustrated with special drawings - was so remarkable that the Princess was offered a four-figure sum for it by an American collector. Other contributors included Barrie, Buchan, Conrad, Galsworthy, Hardy and Housman. In addition 700 artists contributed water colours which were to be stored in miniature cabinets in the library. Musicians were asked to provide extracts from a published work, photographed and reduced and personally signed. As Lutyens' daughter, Mary, has observed, in comparison with the

The Dolls' House library, as seen in a contemporary postcard

demands made on authors, Elgar's task would not have been arduous. Indeed, among composers represented - eg Bax, Bliss, Holst, Ireland, Bridge - are some such as Delius and Ethel Smyth who one might have imagined would have been more likely than Elgar, who had dedicated a Symphony to Edward VII's memory as well as, inter alia, composing a *Coronation Ode*, to demur at an approach to co-operate. Princess Marie Louise claimed to have written over 2,000 letters "with my own hand" regarding the project. If the approach to Elgar was one such, it seems inappropriate to dismiss this as "a circular".

With considerable Press interest in the Dolls' House project, Lutyens soon found himself inundated by offers of contributions. This, rather than refusal, was the chief problem. By August 1921 "all sorts of undesirables" had offered things. "Oh, the rubbish that turns up for the Dolls' House", he complained. However, one notable absentee besides Elgar was Bernard Shaw. In her memoirs, *My Memories of Six Reigns*, Princess Marie Louise makes no mention of Elgar, but certainly gives her view on Shaw. "His letter was not even amusing and ... not worthy of one who claimed, as he did, to be a man of genius. I fail to see how he could have missed this great opportunity to have one of his works included in the Dolls' House as a record of an outstanding author in the reign of George V".

Ultimately the completed work was packed for transfer to a special pavilion in the Palace of Arts, Wembley, in March 1924. The Queen sent personal letters of thanks to the heads of the firms involved in its construction, calling it "the most perfect present anyone could receive". Lutyens received special thanks and a signed photograph. The Dolls' house was visited by 1,617,556 persons between April and November 1924. It was subsequently taken to Windsor to a room specially designed by Lutyens. In 1925 it was exhibited at the Ideal Home Exhibition at Olympia with receipts going again to the Queen's Charitable Fund. It has remained at Windsor ever since.

Ironically, Elgar was much involved in the actual Wembley celebrations. He was asked to write vocal pieces and a march for a 'Pageant of Empire' to open the Exhibition on St. George's Day, 23 April 1924. He took a month to finish the march only to learn that rehearsal problems precluded its being played at the opening ceremony. He was asked instead to conduct his old *Imperial March* (1897) together with *Land of Hope and Glory*. The new *Empire March* and the songs were thus not premièred until July 1924. The Wembley occasion was not a happy one. The rehearsal moved Elgar to write in despondent tone to Alice Stuart Wortley (see Dr Jerrold Northrop Moore's *Edward Elgar: The Windflower Letters* pp.289-90), while at the opening ceremony itself he was "a lonely figure in black".

"Everything seems so hopelessly & irredeemably vulgar at Court", concluded Elgar. Though at precisely the same time he was busy offering his services as Master of the King's Musick in succession to Sir Walter Parratt, whose death on 27 March had been followed the next day with a letter from Elgar to Lord Stamfordham broaching the subject: "I should feel it the greatest honour if I might be allowed to hold the position". After a not inconsiderable correspondence and discussion, during which Elgar feared the worst - "I believe the matter is to drop" - he was, of course, offered the post and duly accepted it in a letter (28 April) pledging "my loyalty and devotion at all times".

It is difficult to explain Elgar's rejection of the Dolls' House invitation. His relations with Lutyens, though not intimate, were cordial enough. In July 1914 Edward and Alice had been among 150 distinguished guests, headed by the Prime Minister, Asquith, at a spectacular supper given at the Savoy by Harley Granville Barker and J.M. Barrie. A cinema camera recorded the event, though sadly the film seems not to have survived. Alice found herself placed next to Lutyens and recorded that: " ... he was nice and interesting to hear about Delhi and I always have a feeling of some affinity to the Cathedral in his Church in the Hampstead Garden City". Indeed, Christopher Hussey in his *The Life of Sir Edwin Lutyens* does point out the "close analogies with Bentley's Westminster Cathedral" of Lutyens' St. Jude's, Hampstead.

Lutyens himself was no musician, claiming to recognise only two tunes - *Pop Goes the King* and *God Save the Weasel* - though his

Elgar's Certificate of Appointment as Master of the King's Musick

daughter Elizabeth was to become a notable composer. He owned, however, to liking Purcell's "Englishness", while his youngest daughter, Mary, recalls that "Elgar was the only modern composer whose work my father liked" and that he was frequently moved to tears by *Land of Hope and Glory*. Elgar, too, had been persuaded to make an abridged version of 'For the Fallen' in connection with the dedication in November 1920 of Lutyens' Whitehall Cenotaph. This he did with ill grace - " ... the present proposals are vulgar and commonplace to the last degree" - and in the event the music was not performed at the dedication.

Dr Percy Young has noted that, at the time of the Dolls' House affair, Elgar was meeting all approaches with prompt refusal, instancing the rejection of overtures from Charles Macpherson, organist at St. Paul's Cathedral, and B.S. Siddall of the St Helens (Lancs) Choral Society. However, Princess Marie Louise might, one would have thought, have proved more compelling. Arthur Benson was invited by the Princess in July 1923 to edit *The Book of the Queen's Dolls' House* in collaboration with E.V. Lucas, then editor of *Punch*. Benson privately described the whole scheme as "ineradicably silly", neither did he form any great impression of either Lucas or Lutyens when they met in August 1923. But, observes Benson's biographer, David Newsome, it was a "long time since he had received a royal commission and he did not refuse". It is surprising that someone as generally careful as Elgar in the matter of relations with the establishment, and especially given his ongoing ambitions for a peerage, did not follow the same tactic.

Elgar left Severn House on 15 October 1921. He spent a few days with Frank Schuster at the Hut at Bray, while Carice supervised the flat in St. James's Place to which he moved on the 20th. Carice spent that afternoon with him, and was also still busying herself with getting her father settled in on the next day. 22 October, the day he wrote to Troyte, was his first full day alone in the flat. He managed a cheerful enough letter to Alice Stuart Wortley: " ... things not quite settled yet as we sent down too many things but you may be quite happy about me so far - the sitting room is in bright sunshine now & looks lovely". The letter to Troyte was, of course, a different matter. Not only did it contain the petulant lines about the Dolls' House proposal, but also its opening was one of utter dejection: "I have at last realised that my dear wife & beloved companion has left me: until about two months ago I always felt - subconsciously - that she must return as of old - now I know & submit".

Can it be doubted that, had Alice lived, not only would she not have countenanced a reaction to the Dolls' House idea which must seem both discourteous and short-sighted, but also that Edward himself would have viewed the affair, and life, quite differently?

BIBLIOGRAPHY

De-La-Noy, Michael: *Elgar the Man* (London, 1983)

Harrison, Meirion and Susie: *A Pilgrim Soul : The Life of Elizabeth Lutyens* (London, 1989)

Hussey, Christopher: *The Life of Sir Edwin Lutyens* (Country Life Ltd., 1950)

Kennedy, Michael: *Portrait of Elgar* (Oxford University Press, 1982 - Second Edition)

Moore, Jerrold Northrop: *Edward Elgar : A Creative Life* (Oxford University Press, 1984)

Moore, Jerrold Northrop: *Edward Elgar : Letters of a Lifetime* (Oxford University Press, 1990)

Moore, Jerrold Northrop: *Edward Elgar : The Windflower Letters* (Oxford University Press, 1989)

Newsome, David: *On the Edge of Paradise : A.C. Benson : The Diarist* (London, 1980)

Princess Marie Louise: *My Memories of Six Reigns* (London, 1956)

Sassoon, Siegfried: *Diaries 1923-25 : Ed. Rupert Hart-Davies* (London, 1985)

Stewart-Wilson, Mary: *Queen Mary's Dolls' House* (London, 1988)

Young, Percy M. : *Elgar O.M.* (London and New York, 1973)

I am grateful also to Sir Edward Lutyens' youngest daughter, the late Mrs Mary Links, for her memories of the Dolls' House project and her father's response to Elgar's music.

King George V opens the British Empire Exhibition at Wembley, March 1924

Elgar's hand-written addition to a score of Land of Hope and Glory *of the counter-melody for carillon.*

IN PURSUIT OF A FORGOTTEN OBLIGATO
ELGAR AND THE CANADIAN CARILLON

How many Elgarians know of the counter-melody to the Choral Refrain of *Land of Hope and Glory* which Elgar composed in 1927? It was played by the bells of the Ottawa Peace Carillon as accompaniment to the singing of a massed choir on the occasion of the celebrations which marked the Diamond Jubilee of Confederation on Friday 1 July 1927. Dr Jerrold Northrop Moore had not come across it and Diana McVeagh thought I might have discovered a little piece of unknown Elgar! Certainly I had never seen it included in any catalogue of Elgar's output, nor had I read anything of the occasion in any of the standard biographies. But it did happen! The performance involved 11,000 participants and was heard live by an audience of some 50,000 as well as being broadcast coast to coast across Canada and further afield. The Dominion Carillonneur, Gordon Slater, has written to me: "The Elgar counter-melody does, in fact, exist. I have seen it! Written in Elgar's own hand, it was one of a dozen or so items spread on a table at the small opening ceremony of the Price Collection."

And now I have a photocopy of this document, the notes written by Elgar into a published copy of *Land of Hope and Glory*, as well as a copy of the music in the hand of the 1927 Dominion Carillonneur, Percival Price, forwarded by Stephen Willis, Head of the Manuscript Collection of the Music Division of the National Library of Canada.

The story begins with a letter to Elgar, dated 19 April 1927, from Cyril J. Rickwood, Director of Music for the Dominion Jubilee Celebrations. It may be seen in the Worcester Records Office and reads as follows:

Dear Sir Edward,

As you may possibly be aware, on July 1st we are celebrating the Diamond Jubilee of Confederation and in connection therewith the new carillon in the tower of the House of Commons is to be opened.

As part of the musical programme, a choir of about 1,000 voices is to perform and the final number will be your Land of Hope and Glory. May I suggest that it would be very fitting if you would write a counter-melody to the chorus in crotchets to be performed on the carillon during the singing. It seems to me that the chorus would lend itself splendidly to this treatment and if carried out would form a wonderful climax to our programme.

If the idea commends itself to you, would you please advise me, and if possible, enclose the manuscript with your letter.

There are 53 chromatic notes in the carillon so there would be no restriction as to the notes to be used.

Trusting you will see your way clear to grant this favour.

Although in virtual retirement (the only other piece I know of that he composed in 1927 was the *Civic Fanfare* for the Hereford Festival), Elgar complied. He had, after all, experience of this sort of thing with his *Memorial Chimes for a Carillon* performed at the opening of the Loughborough War Memorial Carillon in 1923. In a letter of 6 July Rickwood wrote:

> Dear Sir Edward,
>
> Permit me to thank you for your gracious act in writing a carillon obligato to the chorus of Land of Hope and Glory.
>
> It reached here in time and you will be interested to learn that we used it in conjunction with our choir and band at our celebration on July 1st. The performance was a decided success and created a profound impression on the audience of 50,000 souls.

The Ottawa Carillon was installed in the Peace Tower of the Parliament Buildings to commemorate the peace of 1918 and in remembrance of the Canadians who died in the Great War. The Tower and Parliament Buildings themselves had been reconstructed as a replacement of those destroyed in the great fire of 3 February 1916. The largest bell, the Bourdon, carries the inscription: 'This Carillon was installed by authority of Parliament to commemorate the Peace of 1918 and to keep in remembrance the service and sacrifice of Canada in the Great War. Anno Domini MCMXXVI. Glory to God in the Highest and on earth peace good will towards men.'

As Rickwood implied in his original letter, there are 53 bells in all, ranging from the Bourdon which weighs 10 tons and sounds E to the smallest weighing a mere 14lbs and pitched to the A 4½ octaves higher. The total weight of the bells is approximately 54 tons and in 1927 it was the largest carillon on the North American Continent possessing, claimed the *Ottawa Journal*, "the greatest tone volume of all the carillons in the world", though at the same time "as delicate and sensitive as a violin". The bells had been cast and tuned in the Gillett and Johnston foundry of Croydon, England.

Indeed, it transpires that Gillett and Johnston laid on a reception-recital in Croydon at which the Elgar composition was played. The bells had been mounted on a temporary steel scaffolding. Among an invited audience were

The Bourdon bell, with its commemmorative inscription

Billy Reed and Wulstan Atkins. Mr Atkins, son of Sir Ivor and godson of Elgar, told me of this occasion and subsequently recorded it in his *The Elgar-Atkins Friendship* (David & Charles 1984, pp 398-9).

Preparations for the great day were not without their alarms. Problems beset the arrangements for the projected broadcast to be transmitted by direct telephone wires to all the radio broadcasting stations of the Dominion. One test in the early morning of Thursday 30 June revealed that roof microphones on the Parliament Buildings picked up not so much the carillon as the "twitter of innumerable swallows and sparrows as they fluttered about the coping of the buildings". On the question of synchronizing the Elgar obligato with the singing of the choir, Percival Price was sceptical, stating that if this was accomplished successfully, given that the carillonneur was perched 200ft above the choir and enclosed in an 8ft windowless chamber, it would be for the first time in his experience.

In fact Granville Bantock had composed a setting of Tennyson's *Ring Out Wild Bells* for male-voice choir and the Bournville Carillon in 1924, the choir standing at the foot of the tower. This had been accomplished and the Ottawa problem, too, was solved:

Following preliminary tests in the C.W. Lindsay Co. Ltd. showrooms, the telephone was brought forward as the solution, and installation of special apparatus, including a headpiece for the carillonneur, was at once made in the tower. Taking advantage of the radio test of the bells, the carillonneur in the keyboard chamber of the tower was connected with his studio in the Senate side of the House by telephone. The hymn Land of Hope and Glory was then played on the piano and Mr. Rickwood transferred the beats through the telephone by a prearranged count to Mr. Price, who was able to accompany the piano with the obligato on the bells in perfect synchronization. The test was considered so successful by Mr. Rickwood and Mr. Price that they at once decided to employ the idea on Friday when the telephone will again connect Mr. Rickwood on the ground directing the choir to Mr. Price in the tower. The combination is most unique, but at the same time a most inspiring one, and will bring an experience into the lives of music lovers within hearing and radio range rarely if ever known before. (*Ottawa Journal*)

The programme for the Diamond Jubilee Celebrations was nothing if not ambitious. At noon the Governor General, Viscount Willingdon, was to inaugurate the Carillon which would then play *O Canada, The Maple Leaf Forever* and *God Save the King*. After much wreath laying and tree planting, a reception was to be given by the Prime Minister, W.L. Mackenzie King. At 2.45pm the Ottawa Centenary Choir would take its position and be joined by a choir of 10,000 schoolchildren from Ottawa and Hull crowding the lawns on either side of the Parliament Buildings. Speeches from Governor General, Prime Minister, Leader of the Opposition, Senators, etc. would be interspersed with dramatic readings and patriotic songs ranging from *Home Sweet Home* to the climactic *Land of Hope and Glory*. The evening was to be taken up with an Official Dinner, Historical Pageant and a late night Carillon Concert of patriotic airs. Apart from private radio sets (this was the infancy of broadcasting) arrangements were in hand to broadcast the proceedings to open air audiences throughout Canada via public amplifiers. On the following two days there were plans for continued celebration with sports, band concert, dancing on the Parliament Hill and in Wellington Street, a National Thanksgiving Service and another carillon concert.

All went according to plan - almost! Certainly the *Ottawa Citizen* was ecstatic in its reporting:

> This was the voice of Canada, the voice of hope, of inspiration, the voice of the new Dominion, of all our aspirations and all our ambitions ... The hands of the clock pointed to the hour...Far up in the great Victory Tower ... there broke out the clear tones of the buglers. The notes rose and fell clear on the ambient air.

Then, like a benediction, the great chimes sounded. Tense, the vast gathering stood motionless as the sweet and inspiring opening bars of the glorious melody descended and spread. The great lawns shone a mass of colour ... glowing and scintillating in the sunshine of a midsummer Canadian day. Across the azure sky a lone airplane spluttered and swept in circles. The Maple Leaf Forever chimed from the great tower ... The greater Canada ... the Canada of our hopes and ambitions had come into being.

In fact, as the first boom of the great bell reverberated, two pigeons darted from the tower in conspicuous alarm. The "lone airplane" was elsewhere descibed as "a gigantic seaplane" whose "terrific roar" drowned the soft tone of the bells "making it impossible for most of those present on the grounds to hear anything. Even for the guests themselves on the platform most of the effect was lost" and "a strong feeling of indignation swept through the thousands of disappointed people", while the extreme heat proved trying for the vast children's choir. "The heat was intense and to keep the attention of the children under such circumstances for nearly three hours was practically impossible. It was most trying for them to hear so many speeches and for some of them far too long to make a musical programme effective, and those who made the arrangements failed to understand the psychological side of child life...the thrill of the music was lost through interruption and fatigue".

But by the time of the Elgar, the airplane and the pigeons had alike departed. Rickwood maintained control of his vast choral assemblage and liaison with his three assistant conductors, with the band of the Governor General's footguards, and Price in the tower. The carillon music "floated down from the heavens in limpid drops of gold" and, as the *Ottawa Journal* recalls, "to conclude the programme the sonorous tones of 'Land of Hope and Glory' resounded". The choir was "most impressive" in its singing and "perfect unison" prevailed throughout. "The experiment was in every way a success, bell tones of ineffable sweetness and charm adding immeasurably to the effect of the work". It was a fitting climax to what had in the end been a memorable afternoon.

The broadcast, too, was a great success: "a triumph of whole-souled nation-wide co-operation ... a wholesome stimulation of the patriotic impulse from ocean to ocean ... that will survive in the memory of thousands for years to come", claimed the official report of the transmission, publishing numerous letters from delighted listeners testifying to the clarity of reception.

In addition the Compo Company of Lachine, Quebec, under the supervision of Herbert Berliner, successfully recorded ten phonograph records of the proceedings including choruses sung by the 10,000 children.

According to Edward B. Moogk in his *Roll Back the Years - a History of Canadian Recorded Sound and Its Legacy* (National Library of Canada 1975), the Company thus pioneered a technique of recording directly "off the air" instead of in the studio. I have obtained a copy of this recording, covering some 35 minutes playing time, from the Public Archives of Canada. Unfortunately, though containing excellent reproductions of the choir's singing of *Home Sweet Home, The Maple Leaf Forever, Vive la Canadienne* and a number of other items, the *Land of Hope and Glory* is missing. However, I do have the Carillon playing the Elgar melody, though without voices, as a reprise later in the day.

In 1939 the University of Michigan introduced 'Carillon' as a degree subject in Applied Music, and the Dominion Carillonneur, Percival Price, was appointed to take charge of the course. Forty-four years later Professor Price was present at Ottawa in July 1983 when he fulfilled an ambition of seeing his Collection accepted by the National Library of Canada. The Collection has not yet been completely catalogued but, as I have indicated, the Elgar manuscript score has turned up and there may be other items of interest to follow.

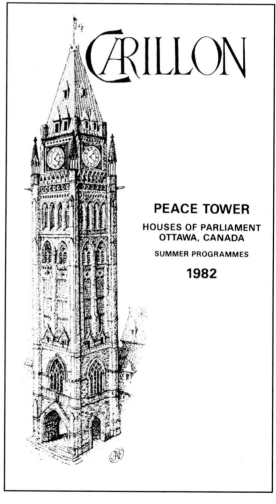

A more recent programme for the Ottawa Carillon

NOTES ON SOURCES

This essay was published in the *Elgar Society Journal* in May 1984 under the title 'In Pursuit of a Forgotten Obligato'. At that time there was no reference to the Canadian commission in any of the studies of Elgar known to me. As I indicate, Wulstan Atkins told me of the Croydon recital which he attended in the Spring of 1927 and to which he subsequently alluded in his book *The Elgar-Atkins Friendship* published in 1984 just after the appearance of my article.

Not much has changed since, though I note the existence of the Carillon arrangement is mentioned in Dr Christopher Kent's *Edward Elgar: A Guide to Research* (New York & London 1993 p194). Therefore it is not to books I can refer anyone who wishes to pursue the story further.

My own interest was aroused when I came across the two letters to Elgar from Cyril J. Rickwood and they are to be found in the Worcester Records Office (HWRO 705:445:3982 and 3987).

I am indebted to the following persons:

Sandra Burrows - Newspaper Reference Librarian, National Library of Canada (Ottawa).

Hugh Davidson - General Manager, Touring Office of the Canadian Council (Ottawa).

Anne Goddard - Arts Archive Co-ordinator, Social/Cultural Archives, Public Archives of Canada (Ottawa).

David Peacock - Counsellor Cultural Affairs, Canadian High Commission (London, England).

Sylvie Robitaille - Research Assistant, National Film, Television and Sound Archives of Canada (Ottawa).

Gordon Slater - Dominion Carillonneur (Ottawa).

Stephen Willis - Head, Manuscript Collection, Music Division, National Library of Canada (Ottawa).

Robin Woods - Divisional Archivist, English Service Division, Canadian Broadcasting Corporation (Toronto).

Above: The 1879 Stratford Memorial Theatre;
Below: Elisabeth Scott's winning design for the replacement theatre

ELGAR AND THE AWFUL FEMALE

I fear that what I have to say in relation to the somewhat suggestive title may well prove to be an anti-climax! But there was an "awful female" - a direct Elgar quote of February 1932 - or at least Elgar persuaded himself that there was one, while the subject does give me the chance to write about a great but, it seems to me, neglected masterpiece. Certainly, of the unarguably great works this is the one, perhaps, least heard in the concert hall, and certainly the one least heard at the Elgar Society's London Branch. In all the talks I have heard there in the past twenty plus years I don't know that I have ever even heard an excerpt from it, and certainly it has never been central to the evening's theme. I mean, of course, the Symphonic Study *Falstaff*!

From the outset *Falstaff* had a somewhat chequered history. Elgar was throughout his life a Shakespeare lover and indeed something of a Shakespeare expert. The character of Falstaff always held a special fascination and place in his affections. The idea of writing a work on this subject had been in his mind since 1902 and Buckley in his *Sir Edward Elgar* published in 1905 tells us of a concert overture *Falstaff* being in manuscript. The work we know, however, was completed on 5 August 1913 according to Alice's diary: "E. down at 4a.m. A. made him tea &c &c & he finished his great work Falstaff". Eight years later Elgar was in busy correspondence with Bernard Shaw about the significance of Falstaff in the Shakespeare history plays and vehemently rebutting what he took to be Shaw's view of the character as no more than an "afterthought".

Falstaff was premièred at the Leeds Festival on 1 October 1913 with Elgar himself conducting. Placed badly in a long programme it was received with "cold respect" according to Michael Kennedy. "E. changed, very depressed after", recorded Alice in her diary. Robin Legge in the *Daily Telegraph*, while calling it a masterpiece, urged Elgar to cut the work by "five or more minutes". Richard Capell in the *Daily Mail* noted that "the audience" had been "chary of applause".

The London première on 3 November 1913, conducted by the dedicatee Landon Ronald, was even less an auspicious occasion. "None present will easily forget the desolate scene", wrote C.W. Orr in *The Musical Times* getting on for twenty years later (1 January 1931). "Here we had a programme conducted by a musician who had prominently identified himself with

Elgar's music; a brand-new work from our greatest composer; a first-rate orchestra, and - to mark the occasion - an array of empty benches!" Robin Legge's review also referred to "a beggarly row of half-empty benches". Ronald, heroically, insisted on scheduling the work again for 28 November and yet again at an Albert Hall Sunday Concert on 14 December. He did this at personal financial cost and without any illusions as to the work's likely acclaim. "I am doing it out of pure 'cussedness' ... I feel I simply <u>must</u> fight Elgar's battles", he wrote to Alice Stuart Wortley and described his action as both "cheeky" and "desperate". Ronald himself was in fact as bewildered by the work as the audiences, subsequently confessing to John Barbirolli in the 1920s that "I can't make head or tail of it"!

Meanwhile the first Manchester performance (27 November 1913) was received in "hardly enthusiastic" fashion according to Samuel Langford, critic of the *Manchester Guardian*. Hans Richter had, of course, by now retired and the performance under Michael Balling was "disjointed and broken". Elgar, indeed, had sent the score to Richter - a nostalgic gesture - on 24 November and observed: "How I wish you were going to conduct this work". "Very depressing time - almost all these days", wrote Alice in late October. *Falstaff* seemed a failure.

Assuredly *Falstaff* is not an easy work and the difficulties it posed to the listener in 1913 are understandable. "I do not think even Elgar has ever written more complicated music", wrote Robin Legge in the *Daily Telegraph*. The work is episodic, quick-moving, crowded - at one level, is there a more programmatic work? Basil Maine suggests as a reason for its lack of appeal that "whenever a performance is given the audience spends the first five minutes in a frenzied attempt to memorise the incidents and the musical signs by which they are to be recognised, and the rest of the time in a confused effort to pick up the threads ... Applied to a work of such close development and musical logic as *Falstaff*, the method is hopeless". There is not even a convenient gap between sections!

And yet the attempt to follow the programme needs to be made. Elgar certainly regarded the programme as important. He went to the trouble indeed of writing a famous analytical essay, first printed in *The Musical Times* of September 1913, which not only makes clear his own wide reading in matters of Shakespeare criticism, but also gives his view of the Falstaff of the history plays: " ... a conception hardly less complex, hardly less wonderful than Hamlet" (Dowden's words); " ... a knight, a gentleman and a soldier" (Maurice Morgann). Elgar takes us through the work in detail, pointing out, indeed, that "some lines from the plays are occasionally placed under the themes to indicate the feeling to be conveyed by the music". He remained, indeed, inordinately proud of this literary excursion: "That's the way to write musical analyses!", he wrote to Troyte Griffith.

The problem about *Falstaff* has been on-going. In his sleeve note to the Barbirolli recording, William McNaught (1964) adopts the stratagem of outlining for the listener the progress of the work by stopwatch! We are told, for example, that 7.06 minutes into the performance there are "furtive doings; mysterious calls in the woods; flittings and sudden alarms". At 7.41 minutes "Prince Henry runs up", and at 8 minutes precisely "the fight begins". At 14.11 minutes Falstaff is "asleep and snoring", but at 19.01 "he leads them into battle". The more recent recording by Sir Charles Mackerras borrows McNaught's notes suitably adjusted. There are 28 cues on the CD version in a work lasting just over half an hour!

However, though Beecham never bothered to reply when Elgar sent him a score of *Falstaff* with a request that he consider conducting it, the work had its champions. Michael Kennedy has written that one may well appreciate "why Tovey the analyst and professor gloated over the score", harmonically and contrapuntally magnificent as it is. "Talk of Till Eulenspiegel or Don Quixote!" exclaimed Bernard Shaw. "This ought to be played three times to their once". The greatest fan was, of course, Elgar himself. Once listening at home to a recording, he observed, after Shallow's orchard interlude: "That is what I call music!" Eric Fenby, author of *Delius As I Knew Him*, has told us that Elgar regarded *Falstaff* as his best work and observed: "Tell Delius that I grow more like Falstaff every day". When John Barbirolli visited Elgar at Marl Bank in August 1933 towards the end of the composer's life, Elgar played some of his *Falstaff* recording and observed of the side-drum solo: "Well, that's a good bit anyway".

The critic William Mann has observed that Elgar's Sir John Falstaff is "a million times more vivid than the silly, amorous sponge of Verdi's glorious last opera". Verdi confined himself, however brilliantly, to the Falstaff of *The Merry Wives of Windsor*, while Elgar based his work "solely on the Falstaff of the historical plays" - *Henry IV* parts i & ii and *Henry V*. Certainly there has never been - Nicolai, Holst, Vaughan Williams as well as Verdi - so wide-ranging a portrayal of Shakespeare's fat knight. If audiences were puzzled by the programmatic detail and musical complexity of Elgar's Symphonic Study, there was yet more! "Falstaff is the name but Shakespeare - the whole of human life - is the theme. A theatre conductor cd easily have given a heavy scherzo & called it Falstaff - but you will see I have made a larger canvas - & over it all runs - even in the tavern - the undercurrent of our failings & sorrows", Elgar wrote to Ernest Newman (26 September 1913). "The whole of human life"! "The undercurrent of our failings and sorrows"! As in the two symphonies and the violin concerto, Elgar was playing for high stakes and baring his soul. Whatever else *Falstaff* is, it is not incidental music. How remarkable, therefore, that towards the end of his life Elgar became involved in a project to reduce it to just that.

It was on 7 April 1928 that the 70-year-old Elgar, continuing the somewhat peripatetic existence which followed Alice's death, moved into Tiddington House, Stratford-upon-Avon, the imposing Georgian residence he had leased from Sir Gerard and Lady Muntz. The area held attractions for him and certainly the Shakespeare connection was one of them. The composition of *Falstaff* had been but one manifestation of his love affair with Shakespeare (N.B. his erudite letter to the *Times Literary Supplement* of 1921) and now, perhaps, he could indulge it. Certainly, he attended performances in Stratford and, since coincidentally some actors lived next door at 'Avoncliffe', he made friendships and entertained. Dr. Percy Young has suggested that in 1927, even before his residence in Stratford, Elgar had written to the director of the Memorial Theatre, William Bridges-Adams, floating the idea of his writing incidental music for the plays. It was, in fact, to be a further four or five years before anything developed - after Elgar's departure from Tiddington House to his final home at Marl Bank, Worcester, in December 1929. Meanwhile, however, he continued to enjoy his 18 months in Stratford, boating and fishing on the Avon, welcoming numerous visitors such as Troyte Griffith and Bernard Shaw, making his sausage-buying expeditions to nearby Leamington. His association with the Gramophone Company continued to flourish, and there were even signs of a renewed interest in composing.

By 1928 Stratford's position as the centre of a veritable Shakespeare tourist industry had been established. It had not always been so. The bicentenary in 1764 of the playwright's birth had passed unmarked, while the junketing masterminded by David Garrick in 1769 - which included *inter alia* a fireworks display, an oratorio and a costume ball, but no production of Shakespeare! - had lost money and left Garrick vowing never to enter the town again. By 1864 and the tercentenary date, however, the railway had reached Stratford and the potential tourist appeal was growing and evident. A festival master-minded by Edward Fordham Flower, founder and owner of the local brewery and his eldest son, Charles, lasted no less than ten days and involved the production of six plays plus *The Merchant of Venice* trial scene in a specially constructed wooden pavilion theatre. Though a deficit of over £3,000 ensued - it proving necessary to pull down the pavilion and sell off its contents - and much metropolitan scorn was poured upon this provincial enterprise by the London press, Charles Flower, at least, was not permanently deterred. Ten years later, in 1874, he embarked on a project for establishing a permanent Shakespeare theatre in Stratford. It opened to sceptical derision in 1879 with Charles Flower having played the English equivalent of Ludwig II of Bavaria (Bayreuth was a contemporaneous project, opening in 1876) and providing the lion's share of the money.

Designed by W.F. Unsworth (1850-1912) of Messrs. Dodgshun and Unsworth of Westminster, it was, perhaps, the only example of a theatre in England influenced by the Victorian Gothic revival. Indeed the structure was, in fact, not so much Gothic as "a mixture of everything from Romanesque to Tudor" and was in appearance more like a small cathedral or, perhaps, one of Ludwig of Bavaria's fairy-tale castles, than a theatre - with its "weird and unsuccessful mixture of architectural styles, incorporating Tudor gabling, Elizabethan chimneys, Gothic turrets and minarets"! A secondary building housing a library and picture gallery was linked to the theatre by an arched, gabled bridge which also served as a sort of foyer since entrance to the theatre was via the separate buildings and the bridge.

This then was the genesis of the Stratford Memorial Theatre sited in what, the railway notwithstanding, remained a sleepy market town of a mere 7,000

Flames engulf the first Stratford Memorial Theatre in March 1926

inhabitants and over 100 miles from London. Heroically Charles Flower, in his capacity as Chairman of the governors of the Memorial Trust, maintained annual seasons in April serviced for a number of years by ad hoc touring companies and from 1886 by equally ad hoc companies furnished by Frank Benson. When Flower died in 1891, against all predictions and odds the theatre still survived. Remarkable as it may seem, although given an elaborate civic funeral, it is recorded that no single member of the theatrical profession was present though Benson sent a wreath. The annual festivals were subsequently kept going by Flower's younger brother, Edgar, on a virtually caretaker basis until the succession on his death in 1903 of his son Archibald - a worthy replacement for Charles Flower.

Archie Flower, knighted in 1930, remained Chairman at Stratford until the end of the Second World War - as long as and virtually covering the same period as that of Lilian Baylis at the Old Vic. His rule was absolute; no matter of casting, designing, finance, etc., but must be referred to him. He was an autocrat with a passionate concern for the Stratford theatre and the resident company there which came into being from 1919 onwards to replace the Benson seasons. The director of the Company was the thirty years old William Bridges-Adams, educated at Bedales and Oxford, an intellectual

Sir Archibald Flower (left); William Bridges-Adams (right)

whose first concern was for the texts of the plays and their meaning - not Shakespeare as local folk hero - with abundant experience of directing at Bristol, Liverpool and in the West End.

The festival seasons remained a struggle. There was a short-lived move to turn the theatre into a cinema during the winter months in the hope of thus raising funds to subsidise the plays. An appeal in 1923 to raise an endowment fund of £100,000 in fact raised £2,000! Sets were painted on both sides of canvases to save money. But things gradually improved. After the First World War the coming of the car and motor coach revolution confirmed for Stratford what the railway era had begun. The market town was rapidly becoming a tourist centre. In 1920 31,000 people visited the Shakespeare birthplace, and by 1926 it was 87,000 of whom 18,000 were Americans. By 1925 Archie Flower had obtained a Royal Charter of Incorporation for the Memorial Theatre, thus lending it enhanced status. Flower was able to envisage a continuous season from April through to September.

But when Edward Elgar became a citizen of Stratford in April 1928 and regularly attended the Festival performances, it was not to our Gothic cathedral/castle that he repaired, for that had been burnt down in a spectacular fire which broke out at 2.45 on the afternoon of 6 March 1926. Its cause has never been established, but the auditorium was totally destroyed - though the library and picture gallery survived. Every available fire engine was summoned to no avail, and the vaunted water-tank in the tall observation tower became "a hundred-foot chimney, funneling the flames".

Jokes abounded about the demise of the eccentric and inadequate building. Archie Flower and Bridges-Adams claimed cast-iron alibis, the one on the golf course, the other at London's Garrick Club. Bernard Shaw, a member of the Stratford Board of Governors, in proposing the toast to Shakespeare at the annual Birthday luncheon less than a year earlier (23 April 1925) had observed that: "The memorial is an admirable building, adapted for every conceivable purpose - except that of a theatre". He now sent Archie a cheerful telegram, urging the advantage of a proper modern building and observing: "There are a number of other theatres I should like to see burned down".

Meanwhile, however, there was no theatre - though there was a season due in six weeks time, the longest yet envisaged - and there was no theatre in 1928 when Elgar appeared on the scene. Presumably he did his play watching at the converted cinema to which the indomitable Archie had transferred the 1926 Festival by the expiry of the six weeks in hand.

Archie Flower was, of course, left with the longer term problem of rebuilding the theatre and paying for it. It was quickly decided that Stratford should have a completely new and modern theatre and an appeal was launched on a quite unprecedented scale to raise £250,000 for the building and endowment. However, 1926 was not a propitious time for such a project and, although the appeal had the support of the three political leaders - Baldwin, MacDonald and Asquith - Thomas Hardy and a host of leading dramatists and actors, progress was slow. In the first year only £29,000 was achieved, while the temporary theatre in the Stratford cinema was losing money rapidly.

Meanwhile, however, notwithstanding the difficulties, it had been announced there would be a competition, open to practitioners in Britain, Canada and the United States, to appoint the architect of the new theatre. The American connection, reinforced by the composition of the panel of the Competition Assessors, was particularly apposite, since it was American money which came to Stratford's rescue. Archie undertook a transatlantic tour which resulted in the setting up of an American Shakespeare Foundation pledged to raise funds for the theatre project. Although there was some subsequent imbroglio concerning the conditions on which money should be handed over, the project was, in fact, assured once names like Rockefeller, Guggenheim and J.P. Morgan featured among the donors.

The Assessors for the Competition, under the Chairmanship of Mr E Guy Dawber, President of the RIBA, and including the President of the National Academy of Design (New York), Mr Cass Gilbert, delivered their unanimous opinion in January 1928 on the more than 70 designs they had considered. Remarkably the winner was a young 29-year-old, untried junior architect in a small London practice and, moreover, a woman. Elisabeth Scott was the first woman to win a major competition of this sort and the first woman ever asked to design a British theatre. Indeed theatre design at all in Britain was a rarity in the 1920s; though cinema design, of course, was not, and it has been contended that Stratford finished up with "a perfect Odeon".

Miss Scott, a great-niece of Sir George Gilbert Scott (St. Pancras Station and the Albert Memorial) and cousin of Sir Giles Scott (Liverpool Anglican Cathedral) had graduated only four years previously. She was quite inexperienced in supervising building projects and, wisely, was to take into partnership her employer, Maurice Chesterton, and another experienced architect, John Shepherd. She was, her distinguished relatives notwithstanding, an 'avowed modernist'. It would, perhaps, have turned out differently so far as Elgar was concerned had she not been.

So far as the assessors were concerned her design had "a largeness and simplicity of handling which no other design possesses". It was "picturesque" and showed "consideration for the traditions of the locality". A mild criticism was that brick facing would be preferable to stone on grounds both of harmonising with the general aspect of the town and of economy, a suggestion which was, in fact, adopted - though, perhaps, after all not to advantage.

The outcome of the competition - partly because of Elisabeth Scott's sex and youth - received wide publicity and the reaction was universally favourable. Problems, however, remained. Bridges-Adams' chief concern was for stage and associated technology. It was agreed that he, Archie Flower and the architects undertake a lengthy tour of European theatres in order to study their stage construction. Building at Stratford would be postponed for a year. The new Memorial Theatre should be 'the most modern and best-equipped theatre in the world'. Moreover when work started in February 1929 there were serious delays occasioned by flooding. Indeed, the foundation stone itself, which was finally laid with due ceremonial on 2 July 1929, was below water level.

Meanwhile Festival Seasons continued in the cinema, while American tours were undertaken as an adjunct to the fund raising across the Atlantic. The strain of all this, together with the job of building a suitable repertory, was considerable as the date for the opening - April 1932 - neared. It fell on no-one more than Bridges-Adams, who in the intervening months found himself not only in indifferent health but also involved in acrimonious discussions regarding his own contract.

Bridges-Adams had got to know Elgar during the composer's Stratford residence and towards the end of 1931 it occurred to him that Elgar might be associated - at least - with the Memorial Theatre and its opening. The theatre had its orchestra pit and musical director Rosabel Watson and an ad hoc group of players. Indeed Miss Watson was emboldened to submit to the Music Sub-Committee of the Board a scheme for the presentation of eight concerts and, certainly, there was some individual enthusiasm within the Board for the notion that Stratford might become an English Salzburg.

In this circumstance, and with the possibility that the *Henry IV* plays might open the new theatre, what more natural than Bridges-Adams should be in touch with Elgar - the nation's most eminent musician, a recent resident of the town, a personal friend and a composer who had already in his Symphonic Study addressed the theme of Falstaff and the young Prince Hal? In old age Elgar was, of course, from time to time not averse to flattery and the suggestion that he undertake some ostensibly congenial and prestigious task. It may be, too, that at this precise time he was - as Kevin Allen has suggested in his brilliantly researched *Elgar in Love* - in particularly upbeat mood following his meeting with the young violinist Vera Hockman on 7 November 1931 and his developing relationship with her. At all events it is clear from a letter from Simon van Lier of the publishers Keith Prowse, with whom Elgar had had an association since the summer of 1930, that towards the end of 1931 there were moves afoot for Elgar to write a new *Falstaff* overture for the opening of the Stratford building, on top of which Bridges-Adams had a vision of the Symphonic Study of 1913 being used to supply a complete suite of incidental music to the plays.

On 27 January 1932 Bridges-Adams visited Elgar in Worcester and returned full of enthusiasm. Elgar at this time had *Falstaff* much in mind. The Gramophone Company was busying itself with the business of issuing the recording of the work consequent upon Elgar's visits to the new Abbey Road studios in November 1931. Elgar received advanced copies of the recording in December - " ... without doubt the finest Orchestral records we have made" - quibbled about certain passages which "ought to be done again if an opportunity offers" and forwarded to Fred Gaisberg of The Gramophone Company the notes he had written for the first performance and of which he remained inordinately proud. Gaisberg indeed was counselled to "*take care of them*" (nb Elgar's emphasis) notwithstanding that their publication in *The Musical Times* presumably made them generally available via any good library.

Elgar, revelling in this coup, played the records to Bridges-Adams in advance of their official release and duly sent him off, too, back to Stratford with the appropriate Elgarian commentary from *The Musical Times* which Gaisberg had by then returned.

Doubtless Elgar once more emphasised the treasured nature of this document - his only copy - since Bridges-Adams returned it the next day together with an enthusiastic letter in which he not only got down to detailing the practicalities of orchestral accommodation in the Stratford pit but also voiced total admiration for the *Falstaff* score and Elgar's view of the plays. He also included copies of the plays annotated with musical cues and notes based on an old arrangement which he himself had been responsible for, congratulating himself that he and Elgar were of like mind: "You will be amused to see how closely it follows your own idea! Yes, of course, I have said all this to people who have set out to write for Henry IV. Some of them couldn't see it, those who could see it couldn't do it. You can't set the human mind on fire merely by taking two themes and lumping them together with fugal correctness. You saw it and knew how to do it ten years before I even thought of it. If I had any real musical education I should have known that what I wanted was there ready to my hand. I don't mind admitting myself an oaf for not coming to you before ... but by jove I want to ask your help now". A certain realism reasserted itself when Bridges-Adams' thoughts turned to costs and the Board, but he assured Elgar that he would "fight to the last ditch" to get matters properly arranged.

The next fortnight saw Bridges-Adams grappling with the business of fighting the Board "to the last ditch" over the inevitable matter of cost. On 10 February he reported to Elgar that, though his "kind offer of help was, of course, much appreciated", there was a reluctance to spend money on an enhanced orchestra. Bridges-Adams had only been able to obtain a promise of "£75 a week inclusive for the Band", having already obtained from Rosabel Watson, Stratford's Music Director, a scheme for an augmented orchestra "capable of doing something like justice to your music" which would cost £100 a week. This plan for 18 instrumentalists he forwarded to Elgar, at the same time as promising a second estimate based on the £75 budget. "Please understand that it is not by any means my cue just now to encourage Stratford in a course of parsimony", he wrote, while at the same time pointing out that Elgar could help him "enormously" if prepared to accept the cheaper expedient - ultimately pared down to 14 players plus conductor. Five days later, on 15 February, Elgar was to make a nostalgically-intended visit to Stratford and precipitate a considerable storm in a teacup.

The first that Archie Flower knew of a proposed tour of inspection was a 'phone call from Elgar on the day in question which intimated that he would arrive at the theatre at 11.30am. Flower hastened to be on hand to greet his self-invited guest, only to find on arrival at 11.20am Elgar already there together with an "architect friend", probably, one supposes, Troyte Griffith. Elgar, moreover, had already come to a conclusion - with or without the view of his professional companion. Flower was given what he described in the letter he immediately despatched to Bridges-Adams in London as "a nasty jolt".

Elgar " ... went right off the deep end saying that the building was so unspeakably ugly and wrong that he would have nothing to do with it". The unfortunate Flower endeavoured to mollify his distinguished visitor as best he could. It was with difficulty that he persuaded Elgar to venture inside and even then "dreaded having to take him through the entrance hall ... for fear he should faint". Elgar was not to be placated. When Flower describes him as "charming but adamant" one may conclude there was more adamance than charm evinced, or that Flower, indeed, was exercising irony, since Elgar vowed he would never come to Stratford again and predicted that he would be incapable of eating for a month! He indicated an immediate intention to wire Bridges-Adams and a probable intention of airing his views in the national press (ie *The Times*).

Flower was left to argue that "even if he hated the outside, what really mattered was what we could do inside" and to assure Elgar of the unanimous delight of the Council regarding Elgar's proposed association with the theatre. He presented Elgar with a copy of the complimentary view of *The*

Times' architectural correspondent, at which Elgar rejoined that "nothing anyone could say" would alter his opinion. Flower ended by pleading that, at least, Elgar should abstain from a public protest: " ... a letter from him abusing the building might just make the difference about our getting the right person to do the opening". It was aggravating, too, that Elgar's ill humour was not helped by an onset of lumbago!

Elgar did, indeed, telegraph Bridges-Adams immediately: "With the greatest possible regret must withdraw from the Festival. Have today seen the Theatre and amazed at the abominable ugliness. It is an insult to human intelligence. I shall never visit Stratford-upon-Avon again." Bridges-Adams replied by return:

> Dear Sir Edward,
>
> I was terribly sorry when I read your telegram.
>
> I am not overpleased, myself, with the exterior or indeed any part of the New Theatre except the stage, which was the only portion where my writ ran, when the planning was in progress.
>
> That is all the more reason why I intend that the Festival itself shall be a redeeming feature, and your help would have been invaluable.
>
> While withdrawing from any association with the Festival, do you think you could possibly allow us to use the Falstaff suite for Henry IV, if only, as you must think, in the endeavour to make some sort of silk purse out of a sow's ear?
>
> Do please reconsider this if you can, but in any case don't spare frankness and believe that I shall always be grateful for the interest you took and the help you gave me before you encountered the shock which has prompted you to wire.

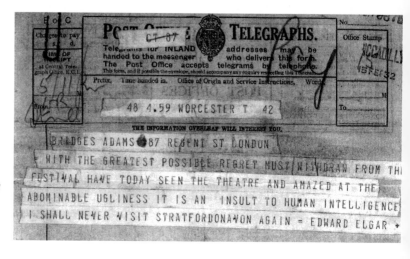

Elgar's telegram to Bridges-Adams

Elgar was assuredly in no mood to "spare frankness":

> My Dear Bridges-Adams,
> Nothing has ever given me greater pain than my withdrawal from all connection with Stratford-upon-Avon. ["Nothing"? The Gerontius fiasco of 1900, Rodewald's death, Jaeger's death, his parents' deaths, Alice's death?] I had looked forward to devote the closing years of my life to music for Shakespeare and I felt that you were the man to see the real artistic side as producer; but I cannot face the possibility of daily contact - even for what might be a short time - with that distressing, vulgar and abominable building. I may have led a deplorably bad life but I can conceive no crime that deserves the punishment inflicted on poor Stratford and us by that awful female.

The "awful female" was, of course, Elisabeth Scott.

Bridges-Adams regarded this reply as "extremely friendly" but "couched in terms as strong as before". Archie Flower was soon in receipt of an equally strong reply to a letter despatched no sooner than Elgar had quit the theatre and repeating all the arguments he had previously put, ending with a fresh plea regarding the potential national controversy: "I feel we can rely on you as a friend not to add to our difficulties by making a public protest in the press". Once more Elgar replied by return:

> My Dear Sir Archibald,
> Thank you for your very kind letter but my eyes still ache from the ugliness and ineptitude of that ghastly and disgusting building.
> I had looked forward very keenly to devoting the rest of what must necessarily be a short life to the music for Shakespeare but I cannot face the possibility of daily contact with that distressing exhibition of incompetence and imbecility.

It was left for Bridges-Adams to seek to console Flower:

> If you take as a personal worry what every elderly public buffer says about a public building, you will end by going mental. I couldn't run my job for a week if I put what other people say before what I know.
> What you know is that a theatre in which you are keenly interested carries the official approval of the RIBA and is none the less 'much discussed' - a word which in the Theatre signifies life. What we both know is that we don't personally like a whole lot of it. What I know is that if the Council had given me ... a free hand with the whole building, as I had with the stage, we should have had a better and cheaper theatre. But that is spilt milk - though not as many gallons, perhaps, as we think.
> So don't worry yourself sick about it.

Worcester

16th February 1932.

My dear Bridges-Adams,

    Nothing has ever given me greater pain than my withdrawal from all connection with Stratford-upon-Avon. I had looked forward to devote the closing years of my life to music for Shakespeare and I felt that you were the man to see the real artistic side as producer; but I cannot face the possibility of daily contact - even for a what might be short time - with that distressing, vulgar and abominable building. I may have led a deplorably bad life but I can conceive no crime that deserves the punishment inflicted on poor Stratford and us by that awful female.

        Kindest regards,
          Yours sincerely,

Edward Elgar

W. Bridges Adams, Esq.

One might have thought - even though Elgar did refrain from his threatened letter to the press - that this would have been the end of the *Falstaff* proposal. Interestingly and significantly, however, there was some further, albeit desultory, activity.

    Having been away from home for a few days, Elgar, in fact, took an early opportunity to write again to Bridges-Adams. Though still "sorely grieved over the affair", Elgar's tone was conciliatory. He was perfectly prepared, apparently, to let Stratford use his music, while himself withdrawing from involvement. He would write to Novello - who held the publishing rights - on Bridges-Adams' behalf. Significantly Elgar observed that he was afraid "the music of Falstaff wd require a lot of arranging - more than I cd do myself", and we are left to ponder this fresh reason, rather than umbrage over architecture, as a reason for his distancing himself from the project.

On 24 February we find Elgar writing to Novello on the matter of the use of excerpts from *Falstaff* at the opening of the Stratford Theatre. Admittedly he would not himself be "personally responsible for the actual performance", but he assured the publishers that "anything extracted wd be well done and due acknowledgement made". He solicits Novello's consent and asks for their view on a performing fee - "if any".

Novello's friendly reply to Elgar evinced a lively interest. They were prepared, given Elgar's apparently generous reference to a fee, simply to "make a small charge for the hire of the necessary parts to cover wear and tear".

Elgar lost no time in tartly pointing out that this, in fact, had not been his intention: " ... there are funds available at the disposal of the management and there is I imagine no reason why some sort of performing fee should not be asked for". He went on to elaborate his view of what would be required: " ... the 'selected portions' from Falstaff would necessarily be used to accompany the scenes in which he appears (generally). A few bars here and there or a short passage would have to be extracted and arranged for the small orchestra to be employed; probably the two *Intermezzi* might be used intact". Elgar indicated his own willingness to consult with the musical director at Stratford.

Novello, needless to say, were not much interested in the minutiae of the matter and assured Elgar that they would be "perfectly satisfied for any use to be made of Falstaff" so long as he was content, and promised that the "usual proportion" of a performing fee would after all find its way into his account.

Elgar, meanwhile, was in touch with Rosabel Watson and, though reiterating his withdrawal personally from the opening ceremony and inability to give "an official blessing", indicated his happiness with the scheme involving 14 players and complimented her on her conducting of the theatre orchestra. ("I remember your conducting of the theatre Orch. very well and always enjoyed the music under your direction.")

Suddenly, however, matters came to a full stop. In a letter of 2 March to van Lier of Keith Prowse, Elgar intimated firmly that the proposed new Overture would not now materialise and that he had had to give up his connection with the matter of the opening of the new theatre. On the same day Elgar also wrote to Novello indicating that developments regarding the proposed incidental music were "in abeyance", giving as the reason that Rosabel Watson had "been superseded".

What then had gone wrong? Certainly, despite the spectacular and typically Elgarian nature of the contretemps, it was not merely Elgar's dislike of Elisabeth Scott's building. As we have seen, negotiations were still in hand, with Elgar busying himself with letters to his publishers, for a fortnight after the debacle of the theatre visit. There is, too, a further question which presents itself. No doubt Elgar, whose taste in these things tended to be conservative, genuinely disapproved of the modern red-brick erection on the banks of the Avon. But does the affair ring true? Does Elgar protest too much? Does the unfortunate Elisabeth Scott present herself as a convenient scapegoat?

Elgar had been a resident of Stratford for over 18 months from 7 April 1928 to 3 December 1929, during which time he had been a keen supporter of the Shakespeare Festival and had struck up acquaintance with a number of members of the Company, including its Director. The outcome of the competition for a design for the new theatre had been announced in a blaze of publicity a matter of a mere few months before Elgar took up residence. Comments, virtually unanimously favourable, appeared in dozens of newspapers and periodicals ranging from *The Times* and *Morning Post* to the *Nuneaton Chronicle* and the *Yorkshire Evening Post*. Sketches of the winning design were likewise printed. Work on the building of the theatre began while Elgar was still living in Stratford, and the foundation stone was laid, again with great publicity, during Elgar's second summer in the town. When he left Stratford Elgar moved to the next county, not the next planet. Are we seriously meant to believe that Stratford's most famous resident had no idea what was going on at the town's most prominent site? Is it conceivable that the first inkling that Elgar had about the nature of the architecture of the new theatre was when he arrived for a look round on the morning of 15 February 1932? It is, perhaps, uncharitable, but certainly tempting, to suggest that one reason why Elgar did not in fact go so far as to initiate a public debate in the columns of *The Times*, was because it would not have proved feasible to sustain this latterday petulant reaction to the architecture of the building as a valid reason for withdrawal from a proposed musical project just two months before the date of the opening performance.

The question of the adequacy of the orchestra might have been firmer ground on which to make a stand. But we know that as late as the end of February Elgar had persuaded himself that the resources of the theatre band would be sufficient. A few days later he was glad to seize upon Rosabel

Watson's leaving the Company as reason enough to call a halt. Since no detailed planning had taken place with Miss Watson, one feels that her departure presented itself as a providential excuse rather than a fundamental reason.

The reason for the foundering of the Stratford projects was surely musical rather than architectural. Elgar toyed with a new *Falstaff* Overture for Keith Prowse rather as he did with the projected Third Symphony. As for the proposed adaptation of the great Symphonic Study, it must surely have dawned on Elgar that such a project was both undesirable and impossible. Elgar had been forced to think about his *Falstaff*. He had been firmly reminded of it by the Gramophone Company's recording. Doubtless to his horror, it must have been borne in upon him that his talk with Bridges-Adams was nonsense. As late as 27 February he was, as we have seen, still talking of using "a few bars here and there", of "extracting" short passages etc. But revealingly he had written three days earlier to Gaisberg on a matter to do with the gramophone records, and nothing whatever to do with Stratford: "I see on the labels Falstaff (temporarily) called a <u>Suite</u> - it isn't that". Gaisberg replied to assure Elgar that on publication and release *Falstaff* would be described as "Symphonic Study Falstaff Op.68".

There are in fact numerous reasons why Elgar's *Falstaff* does not lend itself to ready adaptation as incidental music to the Shakespeare plays. For a start Elgar does not take Shakespeare's view of Falstaff! Certainly he was concerned to present what he calls the "real Falstaff" and to reject the "caricature" depicted in *The Merry Wives of Windsor* but, in fact, as Diana McVeagh has pointed out, Elgar's *Falstaff* is a highly subjective compilation, romanticized and idealised and viewed from a standpoint of total sympathy. Shakespeare on the other hand "neither praises nor condemns but simply creates". Elgar's Falstaff is in truth a partial view of Shakespeare's great original. Elgar, with Morgann, might on thinking of Falstaff picture a "Knight, Gentleman and Soldier" but, one suspects, this would not be the immediate reaction of most people on reading the *Henry IV* plays.

A question, of course, which soon occurs to the listener, is to what extent Elgar's work is really about the composer himself? Certainly one can agree with Diana McVeagh that *Falstaff* is less autobiographical than the Symphonies and Concertos. Yet in so many of Elgar's works involving a central human figure - *Caractacus*, for example, and *The Dream of Gerontius*, especially - one is aware of the composer's self-identification with the predicaments and emotions of the protagonist. Neville Cardus observed that "Elgar creates Falstaff in his own image ... Elgar could not get out of his own skin". Michael Kennedy hears depicted in *Falstaff* "an almost tragic figure who uncannily resembles Elgar himself", while Basil Maine has argued that the wonderful final sequence, which encompasses the death of Falstaff, mirrors Elgar's own growing scepticism and disillusionment. It is music of deepest poignancy: " ... nothing could be further removed from the death of Falstaff than that of Gerontius; yet in both Elgar carries an equal conviction". What Basil Maine has called co-existence within Elgar's personality of faith and fatalism, an on-going dichotomy which pervades so many of his greatest works, may be seen also in *Falstaff.* In the loss and regret of its final pages - "the man of stern reality has triumphed" - the ending of the Second Symphony is mirrored.

The way in which Elgar's view of Falstaff transcends Shakespeare's may be seen most clearly in Elgar's interpolated "interludes", and especially the first when Falstaff has fallen into a drunken sleep and dreams of his younger days. In Shakespeare the action while Falstaff sleeps behind the arras consists of comic business in which Quickly and Falstaff's familiars discover his unpaid bills. Elgar, however, has none of this. Instead there is a 'Dream Interlude' lasting about 2.5 minutes which has no counterpart in either of the plays - apart from the reference in Act III scene ii of *Henry IV* part ii: "Then was Jack Falstaff, now Sir John, a boy, and page to Thomas Mowbray, Duke of Norfolk" - but which Elgar uses to muse about "what might have been". It is a beautiful and typical passage which conjures up pictures of a lost youth and a lost England in which, as Michael Kennedy puts it, "Falstaff becomes one of the 'Dream Children'." It is difficult to see how this passage might convincingly relate to anything depicted on stage by Bridges-Adams' players, and Elgar's assertions to Novello that "the two <u>Intermezzi</u> might be used intact" seems, on reflection, absurd.

Elgar indeed, throughout *Falstaff*, is concerned with moods rather than events. He himself tells us that in the opening of the Eastcheap sequence "no particular incident is depicted", rather that the passage was suggested by a paragraph in Dowden about the vitality, noise and freedom of the London streets. And Diana McVeagh has reminded us that Elgar did not scruple to ignore Shakespeare's chronology: " ... there is no scene at the tavern before the robbery, the plotting takes place in the prince's apartments". One feels that Bridges-Adams' ingenuity as a producer might have been taxed convincingly to blend some of Elgar's presumed interpolations with the actual events of the play. It may be noted too that over the course of the two parts of *Henry IV* there is a good deal more 'play' than there is Elgar's 'music'. Entire episodes are ignored by Elgar and crucial characters do not fall within the scope of the Symphonic Study. There is, for example, no reference to Hotspur or to Henry IV himself, and one is left to conclude that either Elgar would have needed to provide reams of additional music, on top of the proposed overture, or that the incidental music would have proved very episodic with stretches - especially in *Henry IV* part i - of lengthy silence.

Both Neville Cardus (" ... the true hero of Falstaff is Prince Hal") and Michael Kennedy, who wonders whether Elgar was ever tempted to title the work *Henry V*, emphasise the incompleteness of Elgar's study. Indeed, on reflection there is certainly a case for titling the work - as was the case with Giovanni Pacini's little-known opera - *La Gioventu di Enrico V.*

Elgar's *Falstaff* is at once narrower than Shakespeare's *Henry IV* plays and wider in its scope. Not only is it, as I have argued, autobiographical, but also one recalls Elgar's letter to Ernest Newman in 1913: " ... the whole of human life ... over it all runs ... the undercurrent of our failings and sorrows". Or as William McNaught has written: "Behind the labelling of themes and the pages of drama there is a second programme that appeals to a sense other than the musical. It has reached you if at the end of the work you feel a heightened sense of humanity, the humour and the colour of life that surround Sir John Falstaff and his gang, and if in the music you have heard the voice of things English, of London and the West Country of 500 years ago, or of yesterday - it makes no difference".

As a musical structure, too, *Falstaff* stands inviolable. It is, of course, possible to excerpt the two Interludes without too much trouble but, as Elgar testily reminded Gaisberg, the work is not a Suite. It is, rather, essentially symphonic in structure. There is an opening section which serves to present a number of themes (four for Falstaff alone), which are subsequently developed in the passages depicting the Gadshill and Shrewsbury fights. As well as two lyrical pauses (the Interludes), there is a scherzo-like episode and a final recapitulatory passage with a concluding epilogue. The work does not lend itself to the sensible excision of brief passages.

Thomas Dunhill, in his *Sir Edward Elgar*, on the one hand bemoans that Elgar did not "enlarge the scope of his conception" and write a complete Falstaff opera. On the other he confesses that words seem superfluous to the communicability of the work. Basil Maine is not so ambivalent. *Falstaff*, he argues, is "the final answer to those who, with *Caractacus* in mind, assert that Elgar had missed the better part of his vocation in refusing to write an opera. Elgar's is a symphonic way of thinking. The spontaneity and nervous energy of his most characteristic music would have been frustrated by the imposition of non-musical conditions".

Elgar's view of Falstaff, then, was not exactly that of Shakespeare and the extra-musical purpose of his work does not necessarily coincide with Shakespeare's purpose. Moreover the extremely elaborate musical structure of what is virtually a full-blown symphony does not lend itself to what Elgar himself, on a famous later occasion, dismissed as "tinkering". *Falstaff* is a self-sufficient masterpiece, inspired by but not simply mirroring Shakespeare. It is not to be reduced to incidental music and confined within Elisabeth Scott's latterday equivalent of Shakespeare's "Wooden O".

The Elgar affair apart, the task of opening the Stratford theatre successfully and on time proved a nightmare. The Company did not arrive back from its American tour until 24 March and rehearsals at Stratford began, after a minimal break, at the beginning of April. There were just three weeks to prepare for a season in which no less than seven plays were announced for the opening week. Last minute work on the stage itself interfered with rehearsals which themselves continued into the early hours of the morning. The Company was, of course, unfamiliar with the stage machinery and, though most of the plays had been in repertory during the American tour, Bridges-Adams' attempted insistence that, at least, they be presented in new designs led to further complications.

Notwithstanding Elgar's withdrawal and Bridges-Adams consequent intention of abandoning *Henry IV* for the opening night, a late decision was taken to stage the play after all, more or less for want of an alternative in view of problems of crowd rehearsal (*Julius Caesar*) and sets (*A Midsummer Night's Dream*) which beset other suggested possibilities. The two parts of *Henry IV* were still being rehearsed in the early hours on 23 April, the day of the great occasion.

Over 100,000 people were in Stratford for the festivities, the most spectacular of which was the arrival of the Prince of Wales piloting his own monoplane. He was greeted in Stratford by Archie Flower, who was currently mayor of the town as well as Chairman of the Memorial Theatre Trust. Elisabeth Scott was on hand to present the Prince with the key to the theatre and the royal party, in the absence of of a royal box, then proceeded to seats at the rear of the dress circle. The Prince was scheduled to return to Windsor at the interval and duly departed, leaving the performance to limp to a dreary close and subsequent critical savaging. A distinguished audience included the Poet Laureate, John Masefield, who had written a special ode for the occasion. The Master of the King's Musick, Sir Edward Elgar was, of course, not present.

At the time that he was embroiled in the Stratford project, Elgar had had the idea of his composing a Third Symphony put into his head by Bernard Shaw. It was, of course, never accomplished and it was in respect of the sketches he had drafted that W.H. Reed was given the instruction by Elgar from his deathbed that no one should be allowed to "tinker with" the bits and pieces. The virtually parallel project to compose an opera, *The Spanish Lady*, to a text by Barry Jackson based on Ben Jonson was likewise left unfinished.

In fact no music of any significance was composed by Elgar in these last months of his life, though he arranged his *Severn Suite*, originally scored for brass band, for orchestra and continued to conduct and make recordings. Indeed the most famous of the latter, the Violin Concerto with the young Yehudi Menuhin, led to a celebrated Paris performance, Elgar's only flight in an aeroplane, and his visit to the invalid and self-exiled Delius at Grez-sur-Loing in May 1933. In October of that year it was discovered that Elgar had incurable cancer. He died on 23 February 1934.

Less than two months later on 15 April Bridges-Adams resigned as Director of the Stratford Festival Company two days before the opening of the 1934 season. The strain occasioned by the opening of the theatre and its inaugural season had been immense and, though the 1933 season was an artistic and commercial success, Bridges-Adams' relationship with Archie Flower was in irreversible decline. Flower, perhaps understandably after the difficulties of recent years, carried prudence to a point of parsimony, and seemed interested only in spending money on tangible projects which preferably involved bricks and mortar. Bridges-Adams was eager, now that the economic future seemed secure, to have a freer hand in artistic matters. Already in 1932 he had told Archie how much more comfortable life might have been producing for the London stage "with half the frittering away of nervous energy that Stratford involves". He compared himself with a Micawber-like figure who had "waited a very long time for something to turn up".

Bridges-Adams' resignation probably pre-empted a determination on Archie's part not to renew his contract when it expired later in 1934. An attempt to prevent acrimony by offering Bridges-Adams a seat on the governing body had the opposite result. In that final season Bridges-Adams directed productions of *The Tempest* and *Love's Labour's Lost* but spent as much time as possible away from Stratford. The day after the final night of the season, he left Stratford and never returned. He worked for the Drama Department of the British Council and, in retirement, busied himself with writing. He never directed in the theatre again.

Bridges-Adams' departure is generally regarded as having been a disaster for the Stratford theatre. Recovery, of course, inevitably came and there have been the years of Peter Hall and Trevor Nunn, of the adoption of the name of 'The Royal Shakespeare Company' and the occupancy of the Barbican Theatre in London. The Stratford Theatre remains: " ... that great lump of masonry standing on the river bank, imposing itself on everyone who has to work there", as George Devine described it, while Tyrone Guthrie's advice was to "sink it and start again". Elgar had his supporters after all!

Elisabeth Scott was never again involved in anything so controversial or prestigious, perhaps her most notable role being in the design of new buildings at Newnham College, Cambridge. She married in 1936 but there were no children. She died in 1972. Among her hobbies listed in *Who's Who* were music and theatre.

BIBLIOGRAPHY

Allen, Kevin : *Elgar in Love* (Malvern, 2000).
Anderson, Robert : *Elgar* (J.M.Dent, London, 1993).
Beauman, Sally : *Royal Shakespeare Company : History of Ten Decades* (Oxford University Press, 1982).
Buckley, Robert : *Sir Edward Elgar* (The Bodley Head, London, 1905).
Cardus, Neville : *Ten Composers* (Jonathan Cape, London, 1945).
Collett, Pauline : *Elgar Lived Here* (Thames Publishing, London, 1981).
Dunhill, Thomas : *Sir Edward Elgar* (Blackie & Son, London & Glasgow, 1938).
Elgar, Edward : *Falstaff. Analytical Essay by the Composer* (Novello & Co., London, 1913).
Fenby, Eric : *Delius As I Knew Him* (G.Bell & Son, London, 1936).
Kennedy, Michael : *Elgar's Orchestral Music* (BBC Publications, London, 1970).
Kennedy, Michael : *Portrait of Elgar* (Oxford University Press, 2nd Edition, 1982).
Kennedy, Michael : *Barbirolli, Conductor Laureate* (MacGibbon & Kee, London 1971).
Maine, Basil : *Elgar, His Life and Works* (G.Bell & Son, London 1933).
McVeagh, Diana : *Edward Elgar : His Life and Music* (J.M.Dent, London 1955).
Moore, Jerrold Northrop : *Edward Elgar : A Creative Life* (Oxford University Press, 1984).
Moore, Jerrold Northrop : *Elgar and His Publishers : Letters of a Creative Life* (Oxford University Press, 1987)
Moore, Jerrold Northrop : *Edward Elgar : Letters of a Lifetime* (Oxford University Press, 1990).
Moore, Jerrold Northrop : *Elgar on Record* (Oxford University Press, 1974).
Young, Percy M. : *Elgar O.M.* (White Lion Publishers, London, 1973).

Papers relating to the Elgar/Flower/Bridges-Adams contretemps are to be found in the Flower Collection at the Shakespeare Centre (The Shakespeare Birthplace Trust) at Stratford-Upon-Avon.

Letters from Bridges-Adams and Flower to Elgar may be found in the Elgar Collection at the Worcester Public Records Office and the W. Bridges-Adams Papers at the University Library (Special Collections) at the University of Calgary, Alberta, Canada.

Elgar's letters to Flower and Bridges-Adams are to be found in draft in the Letters Books at the Elgar Birthplace.

INDEX

References to photographs are shown in *italics*. All musical and literary works are listed under the name of their composer or author, and buildings and localities are listed under the town or city in which they are to be found.

Also published by Elgar Editions

The Music of Elgar series:

The Best of Me - A Gerontius Centenary Companion
ed Geoffrey Hodgkins

Oh, My Horses! - Elgar and the Great War ed Lewis Foreman

Other titles:

Elgar and Chivalry by Robert Anderson
In the Bavarian Highlands by Peter Greaves
Half-Century: The Elgar Society 1951-2001 ed Michael Trott

The Elgar Society was formed in 1951 with the objective of promoting interest in the composer and his music. With a number of significant achievements to its credit, the Society is now the largest UK-based composer appreciation society with ten regional branches in Britain and about 10% of its membership resident outside the UK. In 1997 the Society launched its own Internet website (http://www.elgar.org) with the aim of spreading knowledge of Elgar around the world and, in the process, attracting a greater international membership. This was followed in 1999 by Elgar Enterprises, the trading arm of the Society, whose purpose is to raise funds for the Society's charitable projects through the publication and sale of books, CDs, CD-ROMs and other material about the composer and his music, and in October 2001 by the launch of the Elgar Society Edition, a scheme to continue the uniform edition of all the composer's music.

All enquiries about membership should be addressed to :
David Morris, 2 Marriotts Close, Haddenham, Aylesbury, Bucks, England
HP17 8BT
telephone : +44 1844 299239; fax : +44 870 734 6772
e-mail : membership@elgar.org

On-line and postal membership application forms can be found on the website at: 'http://www.elgar.org/5memform.htm'

The Elgar Foundation was established in 1973. Its objectives include supporting the Elgar Birthplace, the cottage in which Elgar was born in Lower Broadheath, some three miles west of the city of Worcester. The Birthplace now houses a collection of memorabilia associated with the composer, while the adjacent Elgar Centre provides an introduction to the composer's life and music and a meeting place for Elgarian events. They are open to the public daily throughout most of the year.

To check opening times or for further information:
telephone +44 1905 333224; fax +44 1905 333426;
e-mail: birthplace@elgar.org